SKATE AND DESTROY

THE FIRST 25 YEARS OF

THRASHER
MAGAZINE

UNIVERSE

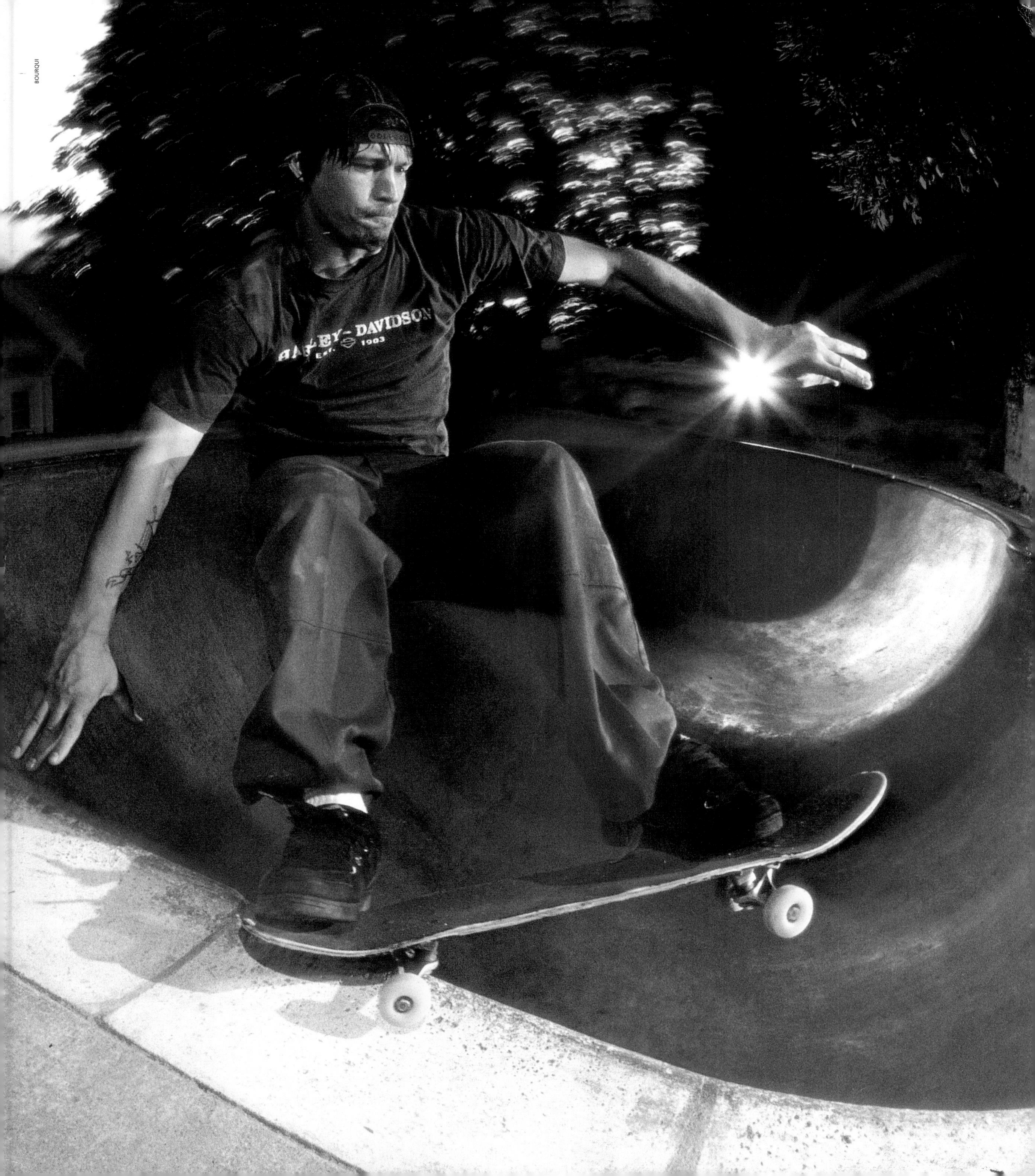

BOURQUI

PUBLISHER Edward H Riggins
EDITOR IN CHIEF Jake Phelps
ASSISTANT PUBLISHER Jeff Rafnson
GENERAL COUNSEL James M Barrett

PHOTO EDITOR Luke Ogden
EDITOR AT LARGE Michael Burnett
MANAGING EDITOR Ryan Henry
CREATIVE DIRECTOR Kevin Convertito
ART DIRECTOR Dan Whiteley
ASSOCIATE ART DIRECTOR Adam Creagan
ASSOCIATE DESIGNERS Jeremy Ortega, Trenton Temple
COPY EDITOR Erin Dyer

FILM SCAN TECH Randy Dodson
SCAN ASSISTANTS Brandon Duley, Byron Ortega, Eddie Riggins
VIDEO ROAM Preston Maigetter
WEBSLINGER Greg Smith

STAFF WRITERS & PHOTOGRAPHERS
Lance Dawes, Andy Harris, Joe Hammeke, Wez Lundry,
Gabe Morford, Rick Sanders, Nick Scurich, Michael Sieben

CONTRIBUTING EDITORS
Mark Gonzales, Miles Long, Dick Pierce, CR Stecyk III,
Robin Steele, Steve Randall

CONTRIBUTING PHOTOGRAPHERS
Mike "Sleeper" Anderson, Beck, Michael Blabac, Wesley Bocxe,
Jaya Bonderov, Dan Bourqui, Brad Bowman, Michael Burnett,
Dom Callan, Reg Caselli, Adam Conway, Sean Cronan,
Lance Dawes, De Anna, Dylan Doubt, Mörizen Föche,
Mike Folmer, Glen E Friedman, Nik Freitas, Mike Gulotti,
Rusty Harris, John Hogan, Brad Jackman, Bryce Kanights,
Chuck Katz, Steve Keenan, Andrew Mapstone, Sonny Miller,
Gabe Morford, Joey "Shigeo" Muellner, Scott Needham,
Jeff Newton, Patrick O'Dell, Luke Ogden, David Omer,
Chris Ortiz, BJ Pappas, Jake Phelps, Scott Pommier,
Mark Rogowski, Chris Rooney, Rich Rose, Nick Scurich,
Aaron Sedway, Daniel Harold Sturt, CR Stecyk III,
Robert Stuckey, Kevin Thatcher, Bill Thomas, Helge Tscharn,
Fausto Vitello, Tobin Yelland

CONTRIBUTING WRITERS
Salman Agah, Brian Anderson, Mark Appleyard,
Neil Blender, Brian Brannon, Michael Burnett,
Steve Claar, John Cardiel, Mike Carroll, Dustin Dollin,
Cairo Foster, Mark Gonzales, Jeff Grosso, Omar Hassan,
Tony Hawk, Neil Heddings, Ryan Henry, Christian Hosoi,
Rick Howard, Marc Johnson, Bryce Kanights, Lester Kasai,
Lowboy, Mörizen Föche, Mark "Monk" Hubbard,
Matt Mumford, Steve Olson, Duane Peters, Jake Phelps,
Ed Riggins, Rick Rotsaert, Geoff Rowley, Billy Ruff,
Max Schaaf, Mark "Red" Scott, CR Stecyk III, Julien Stranger,
Ed Templeton, Kevin Thatcher, Peter Turner, Mike Vallely,
Fausto Vitello, Danny Way, Mark Whiteley

First published in the United States of America in 2006
by UNIVERSE PUBLISHING
A Division of Rizzoli International Publications, Inc.
300 Park Avenue South
New York, NY 10010
www.rizzoliusa.com

© 2006 High Speed Productions, Inc.

2006 2007 2008 2009 2010 / 10 9 8 7 6 5 4 3 2 1

Printed in China

ISBN-10: 0-7893-1386-3
ISBN-13: 978-0-7893-1386-3

Library of Congress Catalog Control Number: 2005908687

HIGH SPEED PRODUCTIONS
1303 UNDERWOOD AVE., SAN FRANCISCO, CA, 94124
WWW.THRASHERMAGAZINE.COM

PHIL SHAO 1973–1998   RUBEN ORKIN 1969–1999   CURTIS HSIANG 1963–2000

TWENTY-FIVE TO LIFE

THERE USED TO BE A TIME. When it mattered. Which is now. Here is the sterling silver twenty-fifth anniversary book. A certified collectable, served up on a platter of ceremony. High Speed throws another bone onto the pyre of potential self-reverential accolades. Increasing the hate.

Truth is, we have no competition. No other skate publication has rolled as long or as hard straight through. And assiduously avoided falling under the thumb of control of the non-skating establishment. It wasn't easy to do this, but we had no other choice. Either you get it or you don't. You make it, break it, or die trying.

Sui generis: the origin point in this evolutionary equation. It occurred when several of our magazine's founders were attending a meeting in Orange County, CA, where the publisher of the extinct Skateboarder magazine described their plans for Action Now. This gossamer gulag gazette featured such "now" pursuits as horseback riding, rollerskating, BMX, and androgynous pop music. The *Thrasher* founders were involved with the riding and manufacturing of skateboard equipment. Richard Novak, Eric Swenson, and Fausto Vitello walked out of the Action Now gathering and vowed to start a true hardcore publication about skating and related things they were interested in. It was *Thrasher*. And these three individuals are still involved, both with the publication and with skateboarding.

Imitation is the sincerest form of thievery. Years back, an article in *Thrasher* dealing with the Skate and Destroy attitude compelled someone's mother to launch a rival publication featuring a saccharine diatribe titled "Skate and Create." She claimed it was her duty to protect the children. The fact was that the original Destroy piece was a multiple-choice affair that encouraged those inclined to offend themselves, and to do so at their own discretion. The suckers that proclaimed themselves as being the arbiters of taste and corporate persuasion are now long gone. Today, their self-righteous titles have all perished via absorption into the never-neverland of the mainstream publication quagmire. Conglomerate titles with their pandering advertorial content reek the stench of extinction and irrelevance. *Thrasher* lives.

Skate and Destroy is a tome detailing the necessity of honing an approach and wrecking it, of embracing the attitudinal stance of never backing off. Within this volume is absolute proof of the validity of this, a priori assumption. Ignorance of history only assures surprise for the unenlightened when it repeats itself. Be informed and forewarned by the manifesto outlined in these pages. Skateboarding encompasses difference. Think for yourself. Dare to disagree. —*CR Stecyk III*

CONTENTS

LEGENDS

BEST OF:

Bailey zings one over the top at Geehi Dam in Australia, by far the most dangerous place in the world to ride a skateboard. Three hours of dirt road—Nowheresville, dude

Opening spread: Skateboarding is about good times, laughing, slamming, and embracing the moments. **Sam Hitz** lays into the Butter Bowl in West Seattle

FAUSTO'S STORY

THE LATE '70s were gloomy years for skateboarding. The urethane boom was followed by the pool-riding craze, which led to the skatepark building scam. Parks closed days after they were opened; some closed before they opened. Skate companies disappeared, and skateshops closed for lack of business. Skateboarder magazine dropped the nuclear bomb when it decided to close its doors because "skating wasn't happening." By 1979 the whole deal had shot its wad, and skateboarding joined the hula-hoop as just another has-been.

Most investors were fat business types who had cashed in on the boom; once the wannabes stopped skating, they moved on to the next fad in their quest for a quick buck, and what was left of the "industry" was shell shocked. But for Eric Swenson and me, skateboarding wasn't a passing fancy; it was a lifestyle choice, and one of the main reasons we had gotten into it was to have fun. San Francisco, CA, had never been the focal point of skateboarding hype, so all the panic surrounding the "death" of the industry seemed overblown. We kept skating every day; Golden Gate Park, Ninth Avenue, and the Jungle Bowl were all still active and happening.

As far as I was concerned, the rest of the world was out of touch. We had our own foundry and my Independent team was raging, so as long as our trucks were still making us enough money to live on, a drop in sales didn't matter that much to us. A few other companies, including Tracker, Santa Cruz, G&S, Powell, and Variflex, hung in there and continued to feed what was left of the market. The boat might have been sinking, but we figured we would be okay as long as we could keep it somewhat afloat. It seemed to me that kids would continue wanting to skate, at the very least to piss off the neighbors or fuck with the school principal.

Sure enough, my office at Ermico was always overrun with skaters planning trips or just hanging out. I spent my days on the phone, traveling to skate spots or hanging out in The City, and my nights were reserved for the fresh-brewed punk club scene. One morning I got a call from Duane Peters.

As he rambled about the previous night's activities, DP's favorite verb came into focus. He had "thrashed" this fucking pool and fucking "thrashed" Taters in the car and so on. I got the fuck off

the phone and wrote a note to myself. The word "thrasher" was all over my head; it just seemed to represent all that skating stood for. I sat there and wracked my brain about what I could do with the word, and how we could put it into play. As I went about that morning's business, "thrasher" kept popping into my head. Somehow or somewhere it had to fit into the skateboarding scheme. Then it all came to me, something simple and crazy: a skateboarding magazine called *Thrasher*.

I ran to the foundry where Eric was working and told him my latest brainstorm. To my surprise, he didn't tell me to get the fuck out of there; he actually thought it might not be a bad idea. I dragged him out of the foundry and took him to the office so we could talk. In those days every conversation was an excuse to torch a joint, but even in our altered state we couldn't come up with a reason not to make a mag. The next guy to hit up was Rich Novak, who owned NHS, Inc., notorious distributors of our Independent trucks and originators of the Road Rider wheel. Novak agreed that our plan might not be a bad idea, even if we were destined to be bankrupt before we started.

With my partners in my corner, now I had to figure out how to do a magazine. I knew that Kevin Thatcher, former pro skater and valued valet of Rick Blackhart, was working at a print shop in San Jose, CA, so I called him and told him my plan. KT, Eric, and I met in SF and made a deal to make KT our first honorary shareholder and editor, even though he had no money. We needed cash, but that was a minor detail, because we knew everything would fall into place. Eric and I invested what we could, Novak put up his share, and we scrounged up the rest from friends. By today's standards it wasn't much, but we got together enough for three issues and then we were on our own.

"Everyone who skated knew Thrasher was made by skaters, no-bullshit articles, good photos, and in-depth, cutting-edge industry from insiders' perspectives."

KT set up an office at Ermico; we made layout tables from doors and desks and bought a stat camera (essential for halftones) and a cheap wax machine to do the layouts. Eric set up a darkroom at his house and also acquired KT as a roommate. Our staff included KT, Eric, Reggie Caselli, Blackhart, Terry Nails, my wife Gwynn, and me. KT did the layout work and took most of the photos, and the rest of us wrote, took photos, and did whatever else was necessary. We called ourselves High Speed Productions, because we were in a hurry.

As soon as we finished the first issue, we knew that we had come up with a winning formula. Everyone who skated knew *Thrasher* was made by skaters, for skaters, with no-bullshit articles, good photos, and in-depth, cutting-edge coverage of the industry from insiders' perspectives. As the word spread, I left my desk and hit the road. From the Midwest Melee and the Great Desert Ramp Battle to the Capitola Classic and Savannah Slammas I and II, the shit was on and we were showing the world what skating was all about. Everywhere we went people were stoked, and sure enough, skating proved that it wasn't just a trend; it was a sport that would grow to change the world.

Over the years *Thrasher* has taken on a life of its own. I've left the editorial content in the hands of skaters and let them create a magazine that has stayed true to the sport. None of us ever thought that skating would develop into a lifestyle that would influence all facets of modern culture. In the last 25 years we have produced over 300 issues, and the skating just keeps on getting better as the sport continues to evolve. I hope that *Thrasher* will always be remembered as the first magazine that had the faith. —*Fausto Vitello*

for skaters, with coverage of the

Our kind of Publisher's Statement

AND NOW A FEW WORDS FROM OUR PUBLISHER

I USED TO HANG AROUND Ermico, sometimes helping to assemble Stroker trucks or messing with the fixtures they used for welding the parts with their Heliarc. Those were the days when we'd go down to the Capitola Classics and then later to Signal Hill with the skate car that Stroker built. Of course, I met Rich Novak early on, as he and Eric Swenson and Fausto Vitello eventually made the deal to do Independent trucks. Also around that time I almost became a part of Ermico. When that deal didn't materialize, both Eric and Fausto indicated they'd be happy to have me participate in their next business venture, which turned out to be forming High Speed Productions, Inc., and publishing *Thrasher*.

I can remember Fausto calling, wanting to meet me to discuss their latest ideas; next thing I knew I was hosting Eric, Fausto, and Kevin Thatcher at my home on Peralta Avenue overlooking the 101/280 freeway merge in San Francisco. With all the noise in the background, they described their plan to create *Thrasher* while I looked over the original mock-up KT had done of the mag. These guys had been in the skateboard market for years, and while we were friends and I had attended some industry events with them, I was just a working guy at the San Francisco International Airport. But the argument made sense: the magazine that the skate industry was advertising in was disappointing them, and they needed another vehicle to support their businesses. I had some money to invest and some time to volunteer, so I said I was in. When they told me

that being the first investor earned me the title of publisher, I was stoked.

The next thing I remember is meeting with Rich, Eric, Fausto, KT, and a couple of Rich's other business associates in some hotel conference room, where we officially formed High Speed Productions, Inc., to publish *Thrasher*. Rich was the ultimate businessman in the skateboarding industry; Eric and Fausto were the unstoppable dynamic duo of manufacturing; KT was creative and had a new idea every second; and the other guys were investment-oriented. Somehow I just knew I could help make it work, so I was happy to be a part from the beginning.

Within a few short months, the first few issues of *Thrasher* were printed on a newly purchased press operated by a friend from high school. I don't think we could have started with any other printer because we were just too inexperienced, but between us we learned the magazine business and they learned to operate their press—and *Thrasher* was up and running.

Twenty-five years later, I'm still stoked to be publisher of the greatest skateboard magazine on the planet, to be part of a truly vibrant industry, and to socialize with people who are my friends as well as my business partners—people whom I have come to respect for their business acumen and insight, and their willingness to fight fiercely any attempt to make them anything but the free spirits they are. This isn't a job, it's a passion, and I hope to have this capacity as long as I live. —*Ed Riggins*

Flippin' it 1,000 clicks from nowhere... A view to a kill

FULL CIRCLE

ONE OF THE FIRST THINGS Craig Stecyk ever said to me was, "I knew you were coming." Anatomy of a death foretold. Working for *Thrasher* magazine had never even seemed remotely possible to me. By age 18, I had fucked up my life. School? Nope. Family? Nope. Future? Nil.

become imbedded in me. I studied photos. I absorbed captions. I knew it better than I knew myself. When he told me of my fate, it all jelled: I was born to do this. He was just sending out the messages. *Thrasher* is an honor, and not something I could walk away from…bad blood.

"Thrasher is forever, just like skating."

San Francisco, CA, is, was, and always will be a tough town. And in the early '80s, *Thrasher* was spawned there. There were skate gangs: Jaks, Jerks, Team Morgan, Team Helter, CBS, YAA girls, Fuckettes— you name 'em, they ruled this town. I was loosely affiliated but always on my own.

Little did I know that after all those years of reading Stecyk's stuff, his words would

In 30 years of skating, I've paid some dues, seen some crazy things, ridden magical places, and lived epic days. Maybe someday when I see some person and I know it's time, I'll tell them, "I knew you were coming." It'll have come full circle. *Thrasher* is forever, just like skating. Remember it in your heart and it will always keep you warm.

Jake Phelps

This pool in SF was on for a while. Lots of vert, amazing spot. Jump a fence

SKATE AND DESTROY

Or Multiple Choices
(Something to offend everyone) *by Lowboy*

First published December 1982

TRASH COMPACTORS. There never is much of a reason. In the immortal words of Olson, "If you lie, you get by." Welcome to the wonderful world of censorship. Apparently, recent activities of Warlord MoFo have once again offended the sensibilities of high school librarians and insurance salesman fathers across the land. In other words, all words will be closely scrutinized from here on out. Passages such as "the clues to the age old riddles lie vomiting in the dark recesses of liquor store parking lots late at night," will never be read again. Stay the course. Try to retain your sense of humor.

(B) non-participate, (C) discover deep, secret messages, (D) learn great mystic truths, (E) become easily bored. By choosing the "correct" answer, the offensively inclined reader can truly insult his or her own intelligence.

CONFUSED? Think how the *Thrasher* staff felt when our fabled editor decreed this assignment. The mis-intentions of this piece were to attempt to convey the essence of skateboarding to the mass populace at large. Sounds like (choose one): (A) an easy task, (B) a total waste of time, (C) an

"The great thing about Amerika is everyone has the right to hate everyone else."

The way I figure it, the great thing about Amerika is everyone has the right to hate everyone else. Freedom of expression promotes divergent philosophies. I don't know who really is offended, if indeed offense is possible in modern society. But just to clear the air, I would like to state that San Diego does indeed suck, as does LA, San Francisco, San Jo, Phoenix, Cincinnati, Tulsa, Mobile, NY, Stockholm, Berlin, Canberra, Independence, MO, etc. (Fill in the name of your town here— get the picture?) This story's format is multiple choice, allowing the reader to (A) participate,

invitation to mass execution. Well, here it goes: Mr, Mrs, and Ms Middle Amerika, here's exhibit "A."

If you eliminate all the intangibles like fame, fortune, contest formats, dorkman screaming off in the distance, the crowd, the pay for play syndrome, etc, the impulse to skate is the only impulse that matters. Choose your own consequences. The modern skater creates his own definition whenever and wherever. Any and all terrains are fair game.

Pete "The Ox" Colpitts, Japan 2003

NOW A FEW WORDS on law enforcement... Officers of the law are sometimes called (A) pigs, (B) sir, (C) The Man, (D) in times of emergency, only when you're having fun. Rules exist. What you make of them is your own business. If your mother sneaked into your room and is now reading this, she's starting to get very nervous. What's a mother to do? Or a cop, for that matter? For the record, I know mothers and cops that skate. Also for the record, I know many of both types who will never be allowed to. See, we all have these rules. Where the new-expressionist skate-type runs into trouble is when our rules seem to contradict theirs. Conflict may develop. In general, cops improve one's skating technique. They force you into carving the right line at the right time. There's nothing like putting down a good snap-back grind over the curb edge and then pulling it back up on the sidewalk right in front of a cop car. Such tactics (A) gain the respect of lawmen, (B) earn instant citations, (C) avoid trouble, (D) create a mutual understanding. Actually, the law types have been known to seek out actual criminals to prosecute, rather than skaters. Enough said; we all know about the others. In a culture stuck on cruise control, the skater chooses to operate in a forgotten no man's land. In fact, the skater thrives on using the discarded, abandoned, and generally disregarded portions and structures of the society at large. Skaters create their own fun on the periphery of mass culture. Sewers, streets, malls, curbs, and a million other concrete constructions have been put to new uses.

The petrol-binging, mass-consuming, power-transportation-addicted society at large clearly has trouble understanding this. It tends to gain insight from (A) managed, packaged, media news, (B) TV religion, (C) spectator sports, (D) massage parlors. What does any of this have to do with skating? Not much, because the actively involved skater relies on his own feedback—for in the streets, the skater is the master of his own destiny.

WHAT OF SKATEPARKS? A park is the response of society to fill a perceived need (usually economically inspired). The successful park is usually the one most responsive to the skaters' needs. Father Bones, the young white bluesman, cites Ramosland in Florida as an example. After going out of business twice, this park now thrives thanks to its new management.

As published Winter 1988

EXHIBIT B. Now consider the mass media's version of skate reality. Check out "Wonder Wrench," Erik Estrada, Farrah, Trisha Nixon, Mr Merlin and the fabled RC Cola pizza woman all riding their skates into mass media awareness. Or hear the tempo change between the sixties schlock of Jan and Dean's recorded tribute, "Sidewalk Surfin'"—with its "bust your buns, bust your buns, you can do the tricks the surfers do"

refrain (is it any wonder Jan shortly thereafter bought his lunch on Deadman's Curve?). In a later carnation, that wonderful poser Joe Jackson masqueraded by singing, "Skateboards, I almost made them respectable." However, things are changing. There are thousands of bands comprised of skaters creating music. Television will soon follow as skaters infiltrate the media power structure. Peralta's videotape (he sells at duplicating cost, so it's a fair deal), featuring the latest, the most, etc, is a fine example. Stacy had it smuggled into NBC studios in an attempt to educate late night TV czar David Letterman as to the intricacies of skate life. So, in an open challenge to David Letterman: Just let any skater into the sacred bastions of NBC Central, and I guarantee you he will quickly change your mind forever. Sound ominous yet, David? Well, the stale humor, rancid dialogues and dog lust have gone too far. We are taking over and we're talking to you. If you don't give us some skate coverage, you will be faced with (A) skaters in your driveway, (B) your typical terminally stupid show, (C) Chris Baucom in your pool, (D) Poor ratings, (E) we will let the janitor out of the drum.

WHY JOHNNY don't surf. In keeping with the ethic of something to offend everyone, we will now attempt to address several of the most often voiced assumptions and questions directed towards the *Thrasher* staff. Our first pearl of misinformation (or probe into the frontal lobe of mass consciousness, if you prefer), comes from the widely renowned Carlos de Fogtown. Carlos, who actually wants to know, asks, "Why don't surfers skate anymore?" In the interest of fair play, we shall now alienate Carlos as a gesture of friendship to all waterborne slime. The one major drawback to Carlos' living legend is (A) low compression heads on the Camaro, (B) he's from Salinas, CA, (C) he only surfs on weekends, (D) he hasn't discovered that business and pleasure don't mix. Enough, back to the question at hand. Actually, many surf types do continue to skate. Apparently this is a little known fact, probably due to the media's lack of awareness. For instance, the surf media types continue to ignore the fact that the best professional surfing being done today is skate-inspired. If you still see surfing as that close-minded performance gig you dreaded through the '60s and '70s, then you're in for a surprise. The skate moves of yesterday are the surf moves of today. When former Australian skateboard champ Cheyne Horan captures the number one IPS slot, he will be the acknowledged leader of surfing. Once a skater, always a skater. Why does the surf media continue to ignore skating? (A) It is controlled by 40-year-old executives who neither surf nor skate, (B) surf mags are just advertising vehicles for pseudo surf clothing companies, (C) sun and salt water have a cumulative effect on brain retardation, (D) they never leave the beach so they don't know what's happening, (E) Gidget was a transvestite.

ANOTHER QUESTION frequently asked is "Why are you guys so punk?" Apparently, even the imagined presence of black leather and studs alienates more than a few. Anyone who has ever met our staff leader, Ted Three, would realize the fallacy of this query. I mean, are argyle socks and Dodge Darts punk? I suppose it can be argued that the mag is a reflection of its readership. Conversely, I know a lot of people who skate who aren't exactly punks. Remember, there is no truth, it's all interpretation. The reason that *Thrasher* is so punk is because (A) punk is in the eye of the beholder, (B) the staff is comprised of studded leather fetish bondage boys, (C) people don't send in enough alternative viewpoints, (D) contemporary youth is disenchanted with traditional viewpoints.

How about the big one always asked by the straight-types. Terms like "skate nazi" and "skate and destroy" seem to arouse images of rampant destructions and social "irresponsibility." Is it really true that all skaters are on drugs? Talk about

stupid questions. In the '60s, drugs were taken for "enlightenment;" now, the same people take drugs to forget what they learned. What are drugs anyway? Alcohol is the number one drug killer in Amerika and it seems that the ones who pose the skate/drug question invariably are two steps away from the cocktail lounge. Pass the Geritol and the Lucky Strikes, gang, 'cause here goes. (To further

> "Skaters create their own fun on the periphery of mass culture. Sewers, streets, malls, curbs, and a million other concrete constructions have been put to new uses... The petrol-binging, mass-consuming, power-transportation-addicted society at large clearly has trouble understanding this."

keep those librarians fat, paranoid and happy, the obligatory teenage sex and denial musical exposés will follow). Drug abuse in skateboarding is (A) roughly parallel to the rest of society, (B) standard issue, (C) what do you think this is, the fucking NFL? (D) not worth talking about, E) pass the joints.

ASPIRING MANUFACTURING moguls all want to know, "Is it possible to purchase editorial coverage?" What is this, "I'm in with the crowd" time, and everything has its price?

To find out if it was true I contacted several prominent manufacturers attempting to score some quality equipment. My first contact, Jerry Madrid, promised to send me a long deck which never came. Big Dick Novak refused to flow a travel bag until I "settled up my debt." That's cool Mr Dick, except you owe me. I called Larry G&S and couldn't get past the switch board. After striking out with the leading truck companies, I even tried some roller outfit in Chicago. Tom Sims returned my call collect. Powell presented me with a bill for a broken Xerox machine (Jay Smith did it, not me; I am a victim of quality association), so forth and so on. Potato Head, who always has a good stash of equipment, told me to try Cash McAnlis at Hobie. Of course, he neglected to mention they ceased operations several eons ago. In summation, I'd have to say my effort at media power brokerage was a washout, but maybe you can do better. If you want to try, just use my name; try Jerry first, maybe he'll send you my deck. This sordid tale proves: (A) the Amerikan dream really works, (B) flunkies have no prestige, (C) skaters are basically honest, (D) you get what you pay for, (E) if you want a favor, don't call collect.

I SAVED the most insulting ones for last: "Why do you pick such shitty photos?" Well, who says they stink? Just to prove my point, consider the accompanying photo of the tattooed biker. Just why is this non-skate shot in *Thrasher* anyhow? (A) To take up space, (B) he's the brother of a famous skater, (C) he won the 1978 Signal Hill downhill, (D) it's an obvious attempt to build up that hardcore street image, (E) he's our publisher, Ed Riggins.

WELCOME TO THE CLUB. Anyone else, anyplace else, how about a couple of parting shots for the censorship board? So, how about contests? Win, lose, choose, don't. So why do I write such shitty articles anyway? (A) For the money, (B) they are the works of a primitive mutant, (C) I don't, they are written by college students, (D) you can't really classify this as writing, (E) because I care about the future of the sport? ♠

1981

"The problem here is a lack
of understanding of what
skateboarding is all about."
—*Kevin Thatcher*

THRASHER
SKATEBOARD MAGAZINE

IN THE STREET TODAY
DOWNHILL SKATEBOARD RACING
GOLD CUP FINAL

ARTWORK BY KEVIN THATCHER

THRASHER
SKATEBOARD MAGAZINE

LAKEWOOD HALF-PIPE PRO/AM
COMMUNITY SKATEPARKS
EASTERN FRONT   INTERVIEW, SHAWN PEDDIE

CHRIS STROPLE
FRONTSIDE SLASH / THATCHER

THRASHER
SKATEBOARD MAGAZINE

L.A.
SKATEPARK
PARADISE

MODERN
MOVES

ASPO
AM CIRCUIT
READY FOR '81

KONA
CONTEST

CHRIS MILLER
BIO FRONTSIDE AIR / GOODRICH

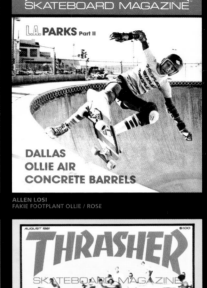

THRASHER
SKATEBOARD MAGAZINE

L.A. PARKS Part II

DALLAS
OLLIE AIR
CONCRETE BARRELS

ALLEN LOSI
FAKIE FOOTPLANT OLLIE / ROSE

THRASHER
SKATEBOARD MAGAZINE

WHITTIER PRO–AM
D.P. SWEEPS IT UP

A DAY IN THE STREETS
A NIGHT ON THE TOWN

COMPETITION: SWEDEN
FLORIDA, TEXAS

DUANE PETERS AND STEVE CABALLERO
AGGRO SWEEPER RE-ENTRY, LIEN AIR / THATCHER

THRASHER
SKATEBOARD MAGAZINE

TOP
SECRET
SPOTS REVEALED

MIKE SMITH
FRONTSIDE SMITH / THATCHER

THRASHER
SKATEBOARD MAGAZINE

CLASSIC
SLALOM

WILD
RIDERS

RAMP
RAGING

MIKE PUST
HANDPLANT / MOFO

THRASHER
SKATEBOARD MAGAZINE

LAGUNA SECA: MAXIMUM DOWNHILL
BALDY: PIPE HISTORY
RAMP BUILDING

ROGER HICKEY AND JOHN HUTSON
DOWNHILL / CASELLI

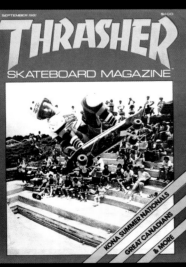

THRASHER
SKATEBOARD MAGAZINE

KONA SUMMER NATIONALS
GREAT CANADIANS
& MORE

STEVE CABALLERO
LIEN AIR / THATCHER

Now 52 Pages!

THRASHER
SKATEBOARD MAGAZINE

Del Mar Contest / Capitola Classic
Magic Freestyle and More!

TOP: TONY HAWK
LIEN TO TAIL RE-ENTRY AT DEL MAR / MARECHAL
BOTTOM: JOHN HUTSON AND PACO PRIETO
DOWNHILL FINISH / MOFO

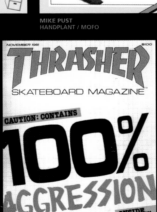

THRASHER
SKATEBOARD MAGAZINE

CAUTION: CONTAINS

100%
AGGRESSION

INSIDE...

"...BY SKATERS, FOR SKATERS,
AND ALL ABOUT SKATEBOARDING..."

THRASHER
SKATEBOARD MAGAZINE

DOWN
SOUTH
STYLE
San Diego
County

INDOOR
BOARDING
A Guide To
Staying Dry

STEVE ROCCO
NOSE WHEELIE / STECYK

Mr Incredible, **Ty Page**

GRAB THAT BOARD

I OFTEN FEEL that skateboarding has painted itself into a curious corner. It is almost its own worst enemy in that it has become over-specialized—almost elitist in attitude. Sure, at one time there were skateboarders everywhere. Enthusiasts numbered in the hundreds of thousands. Parks began springing up in cities and suburbs all across the US and Europe. New products appeared on the market everyday and the skater was hard pressed to keep up with the new developments. Soon there was a professional pool-riding contest circuit and media hype to go with it. Skateboarding even surfaced occasionally during a weekend of television sports programming.

Through all of this, have we, at times, lost sight of what skateboarding really is? And what about John Q-Public, the non-skater, the one who dismissed skateboarding as just another "born again" fad? How many times have you heard someone say "Skateboards?—Yeah, I used to ride them back in the '60s." The problem here is a lack of understanding of what skateboarding is all about. The average individual was never properly exposed to the unlimited possibilities of a platform with four wheels under it—a simple basic mechanical device which serves as an energy-efficient mode of transportation, a basis for a valid sporting activity, and as a vehicle for aggressive expression.

Meanwhile, at the height of the skatepark explosion, the skaters have been virtually swept off the streets and deposited in the parks, where the action is radical but lacks the inspiration of a knock-down, drag-out backyard pool session or a skate cruise down the boulevard with the crew. The fact is skateboarding can survive without parks, but the parks will never last without skateboarding as a whole to support them. Many times I have wired a new trick in the street only to find myself the next day at the park trying to perfect it on the vertical. Skateparks are fun! Street skating is fun, and also visual. The whole world is out there waiting to be entertained, but they want it delivered to their doorstep. So let's deliver!

Thrasher was born out of a need for intense and objective reporting on an activity that has established itself as a major pastime for many people and a rewarding experience for countless others. Thrashing is an attitude, a skate attitude. Thrashing is part of a lifestyle, a fast-paced feeling to fit this modern world. Thrashing is finding something and taking it to the ultimate limit—not dwelling on it, but using it to the fullest and moving on. Skateboarding has not yet reached its maximum potential, and who can say what the limits are? To find out— grab that board! You don't have to be a super talented professional skater—grab that board if you're a novice having some fun on a Saturday afternoon. To the kid hanging out at the Stop'n'Shop with his gang—grab that board! To the college student who needs a vehicle to get from his dorm to class—grab that board! And how about the dad who calls his kid crazed for riding a skateboard all the time—grab that board! There's no rule saying you have to go fast or skate vertical. Just being outside or in the skatepark practicing maneuvers and balance is a lot of fun. Remember, there are tons of asphalt and concrete being poured every day, so—GRAB THAT BOARD! —*Kevin Thatcher, January 1981*

Duane Peters DFL
Above: The first T-shirt

Peter Gifford grinds downtown SF

Well-done ollies early on were very rare. **Brad Bowman** had it dialed. Marina keyhole

Opposite page: In the old days, you were judged by how much air you got. Amateur **Christian Hosoi** goin' for show at Colton

1981

THRASHER skateboard magazine is born with the January 1981 issue. The only other skate publication on the market of any note is the infamous Action Now (formerly Skateboarder Magazine). Eddie Elguera, Duane Peters, and Caballero are one, two, and three overall in points at the Upland Pipeline Gold Cup Series. Bill Ruff tops the amateurs. Patti Hoffman and Cara-Beth Burnside take the women's divisions respectively. Downhill racing rages at Capitola. John Hutson is the man to beat. The first cover features a drawing by KT. The first photo cover is Chris Strople, gnarling a pool grind. Lakewood throws a pro/am halfpipe event, which Caballero wins. Tex Gibson tops the am field. Irvine's community snakerun is the hot spot. The East Coast is ripping right along. LA is a park paradise: Marina, Whittier, Colton, Lakewood, Big O, and Upland–all thriving. East Coast parks Apple, Cherry Hill, and Endless Summer flourish. NorCal boasts Winchester and Milpitas among the living. Dallas-onians Newton, Phillips, Johnson and Wilkes make a big noise down Texas way. Al Losi pops a foot plant fakie air on the cover. Duane and Stevie battle at Whittier. Blender blows minds as a rookie pro. The street is redefined in the Berkeley Hills by Cliff Coleman and Co. Parking garages are the rage. Mike Smith wins pro comp at Colton Ranch. Cab wins Kona. Ramp Ranch rules the Southeast. Rocco and Rodney turn freestyle upside down. GSD debuts in *Thrasher*. Ken McGuire wins comic of the month. *Thrasher* shrinks to 8 1/2" x 11".

Tony Hawk, ollie to indy in the clamshell at a Lakewood pro/am contest. It closed the next week

Opposite page: **Mike Smith** had more style than any surf monkey, and he'd tell you so. Invert, Colton

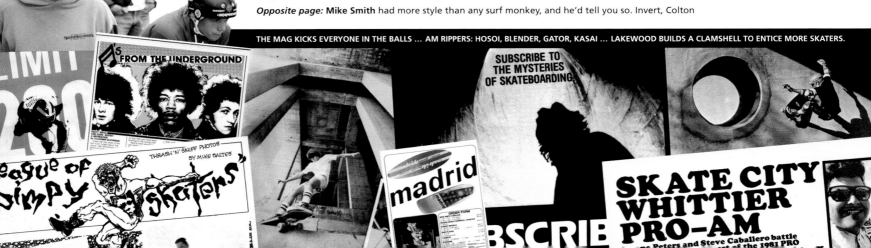

THE MAG KICKS EVERYONE IN THE BALLS ... AM RIPPERS: HOSOI, BLENDER, GATOR, KASAI ... LAKEWOOD BUILDS A CLAMSHELL TO ENTICE MORE SKATERS.

Going up to get down

Cara-Beth Burnside Sweeper, Lakewood

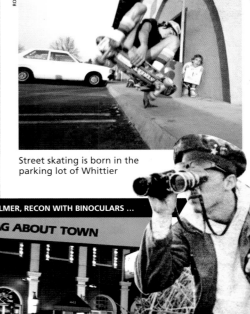

Street skating is born in the parking lot of Whittier

THE RESULT? DOZE IT … THE JAM … PUSHEAD ON RADAR … PETERS AND CAB BATTLE IT OUT … COLTON HAS A CONTEST … MIKE SMITH RIPS … MIKE FOLMER, RECON WITH BINOCULARS …

LEGEND:
TONY ALVA

By DUANE PETERS

I WAS READING my brand new Skateboarder magazine—that I read like a fucking Bible—and it had a section where all the top guys were asked who was their favorite skater at the time. At least eight out of 10 said either Maddog or Tony Alva, aka TA.

It must have been 1976. I had my Foxy Deluxe moped and I was riding it up to Garden Grove, CA, everyday to a place called Green Briar. There was an abandoned pool at some sanitarium that had shut down a few years before. The pool was fucking killer, a wide-opened "8" sort of shape (an Anthony pool) with a spit gutter. Sessions went on every day—and some nights by car lights parked all around the pool, which was tucked back away from the street behind a shit load of bushes and trees. One day I showed up kind of early and there's Warren Bolster on the deck of the deep end, taking shots of Tony Alva and Jay Adams. Someone had put up an extension just before the right hip and Tony was doing hand-on-the-walls on this sketchy narrow piece of plywood, right below the iron hook that was holding the top of the extension board, which was flexing hard every time he hit it. Jay and him were in a world of their own. Completely belligerent ahead of their time, they were shredding the fuck out of this pool, which was called the Fruit Bowl. I was completely blown away and, like many, became an instant fan.

They were both totally cool, and when the cops came we all scattered. Jay lit up a joint anyhow, in my bush, claiming "Fuck these pigs!" He sent a hit my way, the cops left, and TA was like, "Pass the fucking spliff, man!" They skated for about another half hour and then split. The place had six boards up by the time it got demolished a couple months later. TA showed up every now and then, and he was the guy that took every session down. And there were a lot of guys that ripped that pool. Tony was also the guy in the movie *Go For It* that blew everybody away when it came out, and TA didn't take shit from nobody. He was the most outspoken skater ever. When he got off Logan Earth Ski and Alva skateboards started, Tony had the coolest and toughest ads. He was on top of the world and not afraid to tell you that he ruled. And

that's fucking it. TA was the first skate rock star.

It's unreal to think back on how big he got and how deep of an impression on skateboarding he made. As far as I'm concerned he fucking owned it. And if you weren't there? Well, this might all sound made up to you, I don't know. And if you know Tony you might think he's got a big head. Well he does, and he earned it, and he had it long before that! Attitude, my man or woman.

There were lots of fights for talking shit, and snaking anybody who got in the way. I've seen TA go to the top and beyond the heap, and when shit hit the fan and skating was dead he still hung and kept skating, doing shit his way. In '82 Tony, Kiwi, Cooksie, Fat Carlos, and me all went to Texas in a Camaro for like a week. I had to get Santa Cruz to get him a room because the money was gone. "Fuck, man, it's Tony fucking Alva! Come on!" I remember insisting. We got chicks to buy us booze and food, and

Tony Alva, edger circa '87 Top left: TA makes Duane wash up at Lake Meredith

all the Texas guys—I'm talking hundreds—were the most hospitable skaters we'd ever seen. They helped us wreck their own houses and gave us hot chicks to fuck. The Big Boys jammed on the big blue ramp, there were heavy skate sessions, and the Armadillo pipe. Plus a hell of a lot of Texas-style drinking. Ghetto tour.

TA was scribbling every couple days for an article in *Thrasher* about the tour. We got home and I had been doing this chick I called Michigan down in Newport Beach, CA. One time I took Tony down there to party and do some of her chicks, roommate action, and the next time I stopped by her pad TA and a small crew had fully moved into the place. Tony's a great bass player and was rocking his latest band called the Skoundrelz with his little brother Mark on vox.

I was fucking hammered night and day at that point in time, and had been going out with a girl named Eva (who ended up later being the mom of my two oldest sons). Eva would let me drop her off at work and take her car all day, so I got a bottle of Tickle Pink and hit Michigan's house to see what was the latest. Michigan had some bummed-out roommates, and as the Skoundrelz rehearsed in the living room, Daily and

"HE WAS THE GUY THAT TOOK
EVERY SESSION DOWN"

Mondo (a Cherry Hill TA worshipper) are remaking all these cool Alva decks down in the garage. Next thing I know, I get out after a couple of jail terms and go to a contest—and TA's got this whole gnarly crew of ripping skaters from SF, SoCal, and Texas all backing his shit. He's like, "DP, we're one of the big five. Boards are flyin' off the shelves and we're just fuckin' killin' it, man!"

Wow, that was fucking fast! He knows how to hustle his shit and doesn't let anything get him down. I remember an Alva ad from like 20 years ago that said, "I'll still be skating in 10 years and you won't!" He's still ripping, has new tricks under his belt, and is the all-time aggressive soul rider of planet Earth.

ROSE

The Der gets a little reckless on a backside ollie at Big O. This board was what everyone rode: Duane's Santa Cruz with 169s and Blackhart wheels. It weighed about 12 pounds

HARRIS

Concrete in LA was quite abundant and then died early—but not before **Chris Miller** got his licks in with a downstream ollie. Are those weeds in the Lakewood deep end?

Opposite page: True park barbarian **Neil Blender** methods a fatty before the darkness

... FREESTYLE IS THE HARBINGER OF THINGS TO COME ... NEIL BLENDER IS THE MAN ... CHRIS MILLER IS THE MIDGET ... MOFO DOES WILD RIDERS OF BOARDZ ... SCHOOLYARDS ARE HOT ... JUMPING FENCES IS IN ...

A NIGHT ON THE TOWN

BLACK FLAG

BLACK FLAG NEW THE MINUTEMEN

You have the urge to skate vertical, your local skatepark just closed or you never had a skatepark. You could build a ramp, but this costs money, and money is always in short supply. What you really want is something free, where YOU lay down the rules and have full control of what's happening. The answer to these and other questions is, an abandoned pool. It's free. No crowds, no one telling you what to do, and always heavy, full-on ripping whenever you want.

Sure, right, easier said than done, yo... ...re everywhere.

WILD RIDERS OF BOARDZ

LIFE IS A PLAY AND THE

JACKMAN

SK8
SLANG '81

BAIL: The act of falling, either off a board or while walking

BETTY: Any manner of skate groupies of the female persuasion

BIO: To pull off a maneuver above and beyond reasonable limits; unbelievably high air

BIZOTIC: Totally out of the ordinary, way out of bounds, bizarre, extreme

BRAH: Skate bros. An expression showing a sign of acceptance and camaraderie amongst fellow skaters

BUNK: Not good. It may be a pool or a skateboard; as in, "That pool is bunk."

CLONE: To copy or imitate, a non-creative person; as in, "He cloned that move."

DENIAL: To refuse others access to your trip; keeping them dry. Or refusing females access to your affection; as in "I denied that Betty."

DWID: One who is not happening in any way, shape or form; usually describes someone who completely blew it

FACE PLANT: Total face contact with the surface being skated; one of the oldest moves in skateboarding

FLAIL: To thrash about wildly in riding style

FULLY: Used to express complete commitment; as in, "fully thrashed."

GEEK: A highly repulsive person, a pest; as in, "You're a geek, man. Why don't you split?"

GNARLY: A heavy-duty, no-bull attitude, definitely NOT taking the easy way out; as in, "Watch out! He's a gnarly guy."

KOOK: A person with virtually no brains

RIPPER: One who can, by means of a skateboard or simply by his philosophic attitude, take total command of the situation or place

ROBOT: A skater who has no style; a computerized skater

SCAM: To receive products, coverage or favors without really being deserving of them. A popular activity amongst the profressional ranks

SCUMLINE: Usually in backyard pools or reservoirs, the line that designates where the stagnant water was that you probably had to bail before skating

SHRED: The art of utilizing a skateboard to terrorize concrete environs; as in, "He shredded those barrels."

SKETCH: To momentarily spaceout; a mental or physical blunder, either while skating or otherwise. For example, mounting your trucks backwards

SLAM: To make full-on contact with the skate surface; as in, "A vicious body slam from coping."

SNAKE: To cut off a rider as they ride, fouling their whole Karma

STICK: The thing that keeps you going, your steed, your reason for living, your skateboard

STOKED: To be overwhelmed with enthusiasm; as in, "I'm stoked with that board."

TEAR: To thrash (see "thrash")

THRASHER: One who completely dominates what he attempts by his intense behavior and "don't give a shit" attitude; as in, "He totally thrashed that pool!"

TOTALLY: See "fully"

THRASHER: ONE WHO COMPLETELY DOMINATES WHAT HE ATTEMPTS BY HIS INTENSE BEHAVIOR AND "DON'T GIVE A SHIT" ATTITUDE

MAXI: Of the highest degree obtainable or allowed. A term used in the UK to describe the ultimate; as in, "*Thrasher* is the maxi mag."

PREPPIE: Someone bound by a rigid code dedicated to immaculate orderliness in dress and behavior; for example, Debbie Boone in argy

WANNABE: To crave a certain lifestyle or social status; one who wants-to-be

WILSON: A fall of major consequence, usually resulting in severe damage to one's body

John Gibson, frontside ollie in Pasadena, TX

Steve Olson, Foothill Blvd. in Upland

Stacy and the Bones Brigade at Lakewood

News Flash

December 18, 1980—John Hutson of Santa Cruz, CA set a new world speed record for skateboarding. Performing for the cameras of ABC's "That's Incredible," the Hut reached 56.8 miles per hour in Palos Verdes, CA. John tells us the footage is outrageous, so keep your eyes focused on your T.V. Guide for the date in your area, probably to be aired sometime in January.

"the Hut"

John Hutson, the fastest man alive

... REAGAN GETS SHOT ... LAGUNA SECA DOWNHILL ... HUTSON BURNS 56.8 MPH ... GRISHAM WINS GOLD CUP IN UPLAND ... EL GATO IS OVERALL CHAMP ... DERBY PARK

NEWTON

The first action figure who ever came to life. **Cab**, frontal at Kona while the **Bones Brigade** looks on

1982

"Gimme Gimme Gimme."

—*Black Flag*

MIKE SMITH
BACKSIDE AIR / MOFO

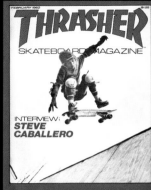

STEVE CABALLERO
FAKIE OLLIE / MOFO

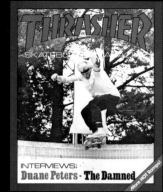

DUANE PETERS
SLIDE DROP-IN / THATCHER

STREET SCOTT
DRIVEWAY FLYOFF / MOFO

"ONLY MAG WE
EVER MISSED...WE
WERE ALL FUCKED
UP ON DRUGS
THAT MONTH."
—*FAUSTO*

STACY PERALTA
NOSE WHEELIE AROUND CORPSE / STECYK

MICKE ALBA
BACKSIDE AIR / FRIEDMAN

JAY ADAMS
STREET SLASH / STECYK

PER WELINDER
POGO / MOFO

RODNEY MULLEN
OLLIE / MOFO

JOHN HUTSON
DOWNHILL / ETHERIDGE
INSET: TERRY ORR
FRONTSIDE AIR / MOFO

TOM GROHOLSKI
BACKSIDE AIR / GROHOLSKI

1982

LAKEWOOD'S LAST CONTEST is held a week after the new clamshell pool opens—and one week before it closes for good. Ruff wins pro, Hosoi tops am field. Winchester dies. Mike Smith and Caballero are interviewed. Cab wins $1,000 at the Pomona World Challenge. We spell it "Pamona" throughout the article. Oops. Lowboy interviews former Action Now editor David Morin about the death of skateboarding. Street Scott is on the cover and in the gutter. Catalina Island is revisited. TSOL is rocking hard. A pro/am series begins in honor of late skate photographer Rusty Harris. Henry Rollins rips on a skate. Malba wins first Harris contest at Upland, earning $150. Amateur field won by Lester Kasai, followed by Tony Hawk, Chris Miller, and Mark Rogowski. Northern Europe starts to bust out. Malba interview over a couple of brews. Rodney rules freestyle along with a pair of Pers from Sweden. Hawk and Mountain go pro at Whittier, end up second and third. Ruff dominates at Kona; the purse is now up to $500. Hawk wins first pro contest in home pool at Del Mar, while Gator perfects the 360 lien air. Ruff wins Harris series overall. Eurocana summer camp in Sweden is happening. Minor Threat is on everybody's ramp-side blast box. Caballero and McGill invade Scotland and Northern Europe. Japan, Italy, and West Germany report healthy scenes. Hutson wins Capitola Classic again. Outlaw park contest in Texas, backyard ramp battle in Florida—the underground is alive and well. Lowboy's "Skate & Destroy" offends everyone, and even launches the other mag.

In 1982, backyard ramps were the new proving grounds. Keith Stevenson built his monster in Palmdale, had a pro contest, and Cab won

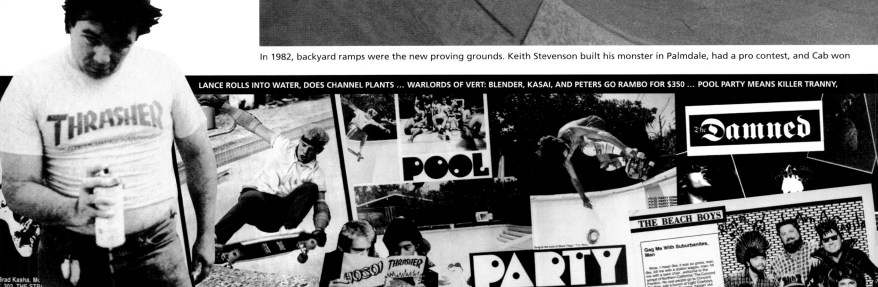

LANCE ROLLS INTO WATER, DOES CHANNEL PLANTS ... WARLORDS OF VERT: BLENDER, KASAI, AND PETERS GO RAMBO FOR $350 ... POOL PARTY MEANS KILLER TRANNY,

STECYK

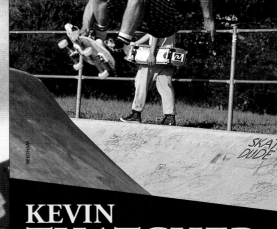

NEEDHAM

SKATE DUDE

it on a cold winter day. Here, **Hawk** rocks

KEVIN
THATCHER
WARTS AND ALL or
GET ON IT

WE DID A SURVEY once—about 10–15 years ago—at a little coffee house art opening showing collections of skate memorabilia, skate art, old boards, some *Thrasher* files, and whatnot in San Francisco, CA. The cake-and-cookies crowd who politely showed up were asked to fill out a one-page questionnaire survey relating a memorable skateboard experience. Without hesitation, little old grandmas and burly dad-types, dorky friends and family that were in attendance snatched up a crayon or a golf pencil, sat down, and began scratching out vivid memories of a skate encounter or boarding recollection. One old lady had gotten chopped in the ankle by a runaway board 20 years before and was still pissed.

"BY SKATERS, FOR SKATERS, AND ALL ABOUT...IT."

Some loud hottie didn't even bother to write; she just started shrieking to anyone, everyone, how her first boyfriend was a skater and blah, blah. Obviously changed her life, for better or worse. A mom wrote about taking a carload of little rippers to one of the first skateparks back in the '70s. A skater wrote about pulling a trick just the day before, but was already over it. There were probably only five skaters there out of the 30 patrons who showed up. People gassed on the old boards, dudes boasted, Betties brightened, moms and babies cried, and overall everybody walked off warmer and fuzzier and fucking stoked on skating, or just by having been included in some way. *Thrasher* mag: by skaters, for skaters, and all about...it. —*Kevin Thatcher*

BROS, AND BREWS ... CLIFF COLEMAN CONTROLS SPEED BY SLIDING ... JAY ADAMS GETS OUT OF JAIL FOR 187, STECYK SNAPS ... THUNDER DEBUTS ...

SK THE DOCTOR
h Dr. Rick Blackhart

STREET
SLIDIN'
by Cliff Coleman

DIFFERENT
BY DESIGN

THUNDER

NEWTON

By JEFF GROSSO

LEGEND:
LANCE MOUNTAIN

The Only One:
Robert Lance Mountain

WHAT CAN I SAY that hasn't already been said? Simply stated, Lance Mountain is the best. Better than you, better than me, and definitely better than he'll take credit for. It's one of the things that make him so endearing. He's humble, accessible, a skateboarder's skateboarder. He's blue collar through and through and punker than you. But he's also a student of skateboarding, a husband, a father. Lance has worked hard to get where he's at: the top of the heap. One of the most influential men to ever step foot on our beloved wooden toy. Enjoy the photos. All the best.

"BLUE COLLAR THROUGH AND THROUGH"

If you know anything about skateboarding, you know frontside inverts are fuckin' hard—but for **Lance**, they're a cakewalk. Full Vari-bot and scumstache to boot

OG City loc **Tommy Guerrero**, early ramp ollie

Edgers: night and day, life and death

This photo sums up the term "fuck it." Sesh is done, the pigs never showed… How about a little buzz on the way out?

FRIEDMAN

Plywood ramps are death traps. **Neil Blender** grinds one into the channel. 12 pros, 20 spectators, $200 pro victory, heaven or hell, you choose

MOFO

STECYK

Jay Adams had just gotten out of prison for murder when this photo was taken. Zipperhead, out of his mind on a borrowed rig

LEGEND:
JAY ADAMS

By STEVE OLSON

ONE OF A KIND
As real as it gets
For better or worse
Not to try, is to be.
Low down, is that style?
That's right, most don't know,
never have, never will.
Mr Adams, from the start
has and will, fuck it up.
Forever.
Failing successfully, go figure
failing, success, what is it?
Jay is success,
cheating death,
living life to the fullest.
Guess what? He has.
What most wish they had!
Whoever wrote the rules,
Mr Adams broke them.
A life most would not be able to handle…
a way of life only Jay can deal with.
The best of all is the right answer
surfer-skater-punker-madman
never to be copied.
Some have tried,
cheap imitations.
Fuck all this bullshit, that's the way
to deal with all this jive-ass shit.
Jay Adams fucking rocks.

"AS REAL AS IT GETS"

Henry rocked **Black Flag,** and the music is timeless. Damaged, life's pain and misery runs deep

… DEL 13 TALKS SHOP … RICHARD ARMIJO TELLS BIKERS TO FUCK OFF … MALBA GETS THE BRICKS ON MISSION STREET … KONA KEEPS ON ROLLING …

FOLMER

LEGEND:
LESTER KASAI

By NEIL BLENDER

LESTER KASAI IS EPIC. How else can you explain the benihana? Or its counterpart, the benibongo? The height attained at events and non-events alike, the power, the style, the maneuvers being produced (like the short-lived, highly memorable Frankie Goes to Fakie, a backside air tweak to fakie). For more info on this see Darren Navarrette (melon fakie) or the Poliki (a layback air, but grab the outside rail; more widely known as an underplant) by Craig Johnson.

The vert wars of this time were incredible. Some had the lines, others wanted showtime. All-time crowd fave **Lester Kasai** grits his teeth on a whopper. For him, it was make it or die. Notice how everyone in the photo is watching him

TA, Fritz Coy, Tony Blue Tile—**Alva** merged the gap between skating and Fuck Off. Thruster, Ammo Pipe

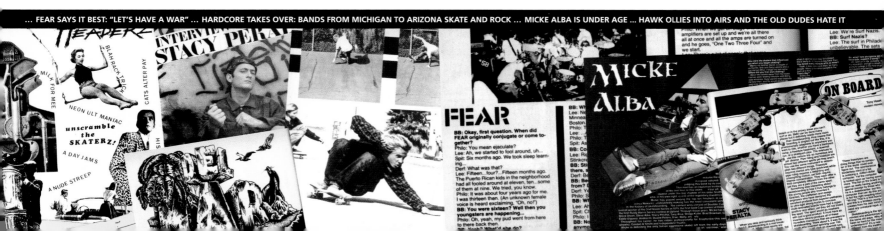

START IT OFF with a bang and keep their ears ringing 'til the end

1983

"People that smoke and drink are fake."

—*Lance Mountain*

LANCE MOUNTAIN
BACKSIDE AIR / FRIEDMAN

BOB DENIKE
FRONTSIDE LAP OVER / ETHERIDGE

BILLY RUFF
BACKSIDE AIR / THATCHER

MICKE ALBA
HANDPLANT / FRIEDMAN

GARRY DAVIS
FRONTSIDE BONELESS / RAMSAY

ANDY KESSLER
ONE FOOT NOSE WHEELIE / BOCXE

JAY "ALABAMY"
FRONTSIDE OLLIE / FRIEDMAN

STEVE CABALLERO
FRONTSIDE CHANNEL PLANT / MOFO

TOP LEFT: **MIKE MCGILL**
BACKSIDE AIR / SCHMITT

TOP RIGHT: **CRAIG JOHNSON**
FRONTSIDE AIR / NEWTON

BOTTOM LEFT: **JOHN GIBSON**
FRONTSIDE AIR / NEWTON

CENTER: **JAY CABLER**
LOOSE FRONTSIDE EDGE OUT / NEWTON

BOTTOM RIGHT: **ANONYMOUS**
STREET PUSH / NEWTON

PUKER AND **PAT CLARKE**
FRONTSIDE GRIND, BACKSIDE AIR / FRIEDMAN

ROB ROSKOPP
SWEEPER / SCHNEIDER

BIG STEVE
FRONTSIDE GRIND / MOFO

1983

LANCE MOUNTAIN KICKS OFF the New Year in an interview. Mike Chantry's Mile High ramp is the prime choice of vacationing skaters. Snowboarding gains steam amongst the skate set. Mike McGill wins a cold Christmas Classic at Pipeline. Christian bomb drops off Cab's roof into the ramp. Steve Alba interviewed. Our Ramp Plans issue sells out. Pros draw skatetoons for the mag. Blender wins Skate City Whittier's final contest. Billy Ruff talks turkey. Alva flips off Friedman in "How To" photo spread. Skate Rock rears its ugly head. Vertical boardslides? Talk to Al Losi. Great Desert Ramp Battle, the first pro ramp duel. Street skating busts wide open. Tony Hawk dominates Del Mar's keyhole and the Spring Nationals. Welinder beats Rodney in freestyle finals. Skate comix are the rage. Stecyk's street style sequentials blow minds and upset parents all over the land. Tommy Guerrero wins the first pro street style event as an amateur and upsets everybody. The East Coast continues to thaw out with ripping skating going down. The SF Jaks team patrols the streets of the city. Joe Lopes' Ramp Jam is the first pro event of its kind. Caballero takes the cash there and at the Summer World Series contest at Upland. Lance Mountain's Manor ramp is the desired session spot. Top CASL amateurs: Steadham, Nash, Grosso, Staab, and Lucero.

MILLER

Caballero means "gentleman" in Spanish, and if anyone embodied that nomenclature it's Stevie. This pint-sized dude absolutely ruled everything he rode

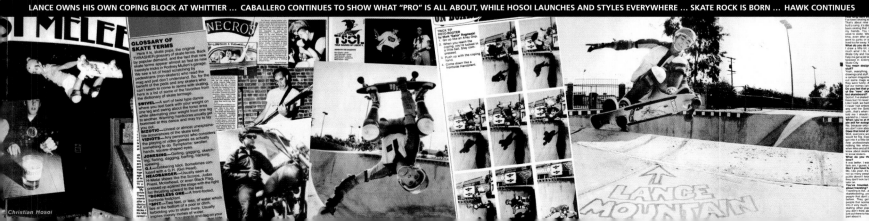

Every good sesh needs **Bettys** to show off for

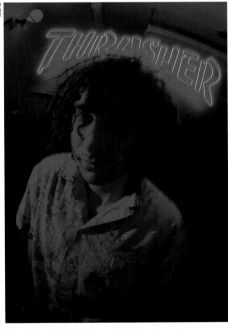

Tony Alva, light at the end of the tunnel

Christian Hosoi was the dude born to blast. His air rotations were simply beautiful; you try doing six backside airs in a row, each one higher than the one before, finishing off the line with a head-high lien. No wonder they call him Christ

TO BLOW DOORS ... TSOL SKATE ... CODE OF HONOR RIP ... HACKETT SLASHES ... GATOR GETS ROTO-ROOTER ... CHRISTIAN AIRS TO FAKIE OVER THE CHANNEL ... TOMMY G WINS PRO CONTEST IN SF AS AN AM ...

LEGEND: BILLY RUFF

By STEVE CLAAR

BILLY RUFF IS ONE of those people (everybody knows one) who are just really good at anything they do. In the early '80s he was winning contests or at least in the top five every time. During that time, new tricks were being discovered almost daily and to stay current was a lot of work. At the same time there was very little money in skateboarding, even for the top pros of the day, and Billy needed money to live. Had the big bucks of today been there all along, he might still be winning contests. His skating was simple—blazing speed, super consistency, and a clean bulletproof style. But, what was good for first, second, or third place in '82 was only good for tenth or so in '86. And Billy just wasn't interested in tenth place. I'll remember Billy Ruff as one of skateboarding's all time greats in a time when the outside world couldn't have cared less about skateboarding.

Billy Ruff was the main threat against Cab in any contest. Smooth, consistent, stylish, and he stayed on. Ruff was always in the Top Five

"BLAZING SPEED SUPER CONSISTENCY AND A CLEAN BULLETPROOF STYLE"

NEWTON

"LET'S HOPE WE GET TO SEE IT ALL OVER AGAIN"

GULOTTI

Duane Peters: Mess, champ, legend. He'd be drinking beers in the parking lot, they'd call his name, and he'd come in and win the thing. If even half the stories are true, let's hope we get to see it all over again

MOFO

Texans are a hearty breed, and **Craig Johnson** is a beast. Early street hip flight… And skating is everywhere

Beers, bowls, and Barneys. Thought it wasn't?

… ROB ROSKOPP SHOCKS THE WORLD AT JOE LOPES' RAMP JAM … CAB WINS … PUERTO RICO COMES INTO PHOTO-G …   MERCYFUL FATE PRAISE SATAN … GATOR LOSES SOME TEETH

1984

"I guess we were always looking for trouble."

—*Tony Alva*

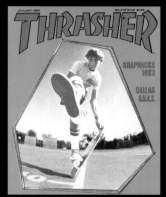

RODNEY MULLEN
ONE-FOOT POGO / FRIEDMAN

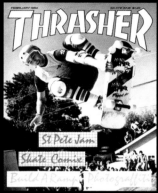

MONTY NOLDER
GAY TWIST / NEWTON

MONDO
FRONTSIDE GRIND / ETHERIDGE

BRYCE KANIGHTS
FRONTSIDE AIR / ETHERIDGE

CHUCK TREECE
LAYBACK TAILSLIDE / FRIEDMAN

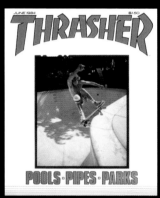

MARK ROGOWSKI
FRONTSIDE GRIND / THATCHER

TOMMY GUERRERO
FAST PLANT / THATCHER

CHRISTIAN HOSOI
BACKSIDE AIR / MOFO

NATAS KAUPAS
WALLWALK / STECYK

BOB DENIKE
PUSH / FLÜITT

(INSET) **NEIL BLENDER**
EGGPLANT / MOFO

MARK GONZALES
FRONTSIDE BONELESS / MOFO

SAN JOSE NAVAHO
ARTWORK BY CHRIS BUCHINSKY

1984

RODNEY MULLEN IS DOING the "impossible." Schoolyards are back in session. In Texas, the word is "shut up and skate." Jeff Phillips is blowing minds. Upland hosts a Turkey Shoot and Lance Mountain beats all comers. The St Pete Jam brings the backyard contest back to where it all started: Grigley's backyard. Bonnie Blouin skins a found bobcat carcass in her hotel room. Neil Blender wins with Monty Nolder right behind him. Craig Johnson sweeps am honors. West Germany rages with skaters like Claus Grabke, Martin Van Doren and Thomas Keller. "Skarfing Material" makes its debut. Agent Orange are at the top of the skate rock charts. Rodney Mullen speaks when spoken to. Roskopp takes a board to the skull at Joe's. The three P's—pool, park, and pipe—are available to the hungry skater. Nails, McClure, Talldog, Ancell and Skipper make a skate vehicle out of mom's sedan. Mark Rogowski wins the ill-named Skateboard Olympics at Del Mar. The 'zine scene is happening big time. Tony Hawk wins again on the right coast at the Kona Ramp Meet in Jacksonville. Tony does finger flip airs among other tricks. The NSA brings freestyle and street style back to Golden Gate Park in SF. Lucero is hit by a car while skating to the event. Natas Kaupas typifies the new breed and graces the cover, skating a wall in Venice. Britt Parrot, Joe Bowers, Batmite, and Doug Walker host a backyard session in Tennessee. A Massacre at Mile High ramp is not without incident. Billy Ruff wins again. Blender is second. NSA actually pulls a contest at the Venice Pavilion, freestyle only. Kevin Harris wins. Yet another pool event at Del Mar. Yes, it's the Hawk Man in first. The Capitola Classic is now street style, and Caballero is champion. JFA chronicle their annual cross-country tour. Mike McGill's McTwist is definitely not for everybody.

Never one to write down his tricks, **Neil Blender** made them up as he went. Gay Twist, Fall Guy, Woolly Mammoth, Jolly Mamba… One of the most indelible characters in all of skating. Another thing: This could be an egg, but it's a frontal

Opposite page: Mile High, eight-foot trannys, downhill, dead cat toss on the flatbottom, fireworks—NorCal, bitch. **Chris Miller**, styled to the max

NEWTON

John Grigley at the St Pete Ramp Jam. Backyards in the cuts? Termites loved it

MOFO

At age 13, **Micke Alba** was the top skater in the world. At Upland, he was unstoppable— backside blast

This is the best photo taken on the day skating changed. **Mark Gonzales** ollied off a wedge ramp and, well, after that things got gnarbuckle. Embarcadero, San Diego, 1984—think about it. Where the fuck were you?

OMER

"AFTER THAT, THINGS GOT GNARBUCKLE"

Sweeper channels are either make or break. **Rob Roskopp** delivers the goods in St Pete. Oh yeah, he won this channel battle

Upland Combi was for real—**Neil Blender** was the only one to monorail through the corners… OK, copers helped

... EMBARCADERO, SD, 1984 CONTEST: CURBS, STREET, BENCHES ... OLLIES ARE UNLEASHED ... TG GETS FREE BEER ... HOLMES RIDES FOR TA ... PUSHEAD MUTE FOOTPLANT TO FAKIE IN BOISE, SEPTIC DEATH IS HIS BAND ...

CHRISTIAN'S STYLE IS ETERNAL"

LEGEND: CHRISTIAN HOSOI

By TONY HAWK

CHRISTIAN HOSOI IS ONE of the few skating legends that have stood the test of time. Tricks come and go, but Christian's style is eternal. I know from experience; competing against him in the '80s was like competing against a legion of passionate fans. While I was trying to learn new tricks, Holmes was figuring out how to blast higher and take existing tricks to new levels. Our styles were very different, and we created a Great Divide in followers—so much that we would get heckled by opposing fans during contests. The funny thing is that we skated together often, bounced ideas off each other, and considered ourselves friends. We didn't buy into the perceived rivalry; we just did our own things. It was an amazing time in skating, and Christian was a revolutionary. In fact, Hosoi is one of few names that people remember from the '80s—just ask your dad who used to skate—and they still hold his name in reverence.

One of the biggest disappointments in skateboarding's latest surge was that Christian wasn't present to add his flair in the beginning. Thankfully, he was recently released from his dark days and you can see that the fire is still burning brightly. He is now free to skate again, free to inspire again, and free to accomplish whatever he might have missed along the way. His style is still unmistakable and one that will never be duplicated. Icon status is not easy to earn in skateboarding, but Christian reserved that title long ago. His skating is timeless. I can't wait to see what he has in store for us.

MOFO

THOSE EARLY DAYS at *Thrasher* were a time when almost anything could happen. Naïve as I was to the ways of the world, I saw the position entrusted to me as a special responsibility, a special mission of sorts. I didn't know squat about publishing a magazine, but I did know a little about taking photos, so with that, and armed with a vivid imagination, I made things up as I went along. There were blank pages to fill and usually the first things that came to mind went onto those pages.

"I DIDN'T KNOW SQUAT ABOUT PUBLISHING A MAGAZINE"

Traveling was a large part of the game, beginning in the back of Fausto's Volvo, then long hauls on a Greyhound bus with a bottle of Peppermint Schnapps and burrito roaches as my traveling companions. Once we could afford it, I was shuttling across the country on an airplane to cities I never imagined I'd visit.

The most important thing I'll carry with me forever was the privilege of witnessing incredible things. By this I mean the skating and the guys (you know who you are), the pioneers who ushered in the craft, taking it from the seeds planted in the late '70s, developing it and refining it throughout the '80s, driving it to what it exploded into in the '90s, and consequently laying the foundation of what skate practitioners enjoy today. I'm honored that I was the person who documented on film and through words the feats that were conveyed to a diverse audience of nations of skateboarders. —*Mofo*

Hawk and **Hosoi**, style vs tricks. The wars that went down at Del Mar in front of 200 people to this day are like Foreman vs Ali. They were always #1 and #2—Indy for Hosoi, Japan for Hawk

... TRAVELS IN OZ PROVE TO BE HEALTHY TO YOUR HAZARDS ... SUICIDAL ROCKED ... AIRS ARE EVERYWHERE ... RODNEY MULLEN BUSTS THE KICKFLIP, THEN KNOWN AS THE OLLIE FLIP ... TONY ALVA TELLS IT LIKE IT IS ...

Gator was all good. This frontal in the round at Upland is classic form

Billy Beauregard, doin' an air to fakie at Kona, had hearts stopping all over the Swamp Land—where his finger is pointing

Opposite page: More backyard madness. This is at **Lance**'s, and it pretty much sums up the whole era: **Mike Smith** (mouth open), **Steadham** (sitting down), **Hawk** (with Squeeb, reading the mag), **Mike McGill** (with a Nosebone), and **Jeff Grosso** (gettin' higher)

Rare Andrecht channel photo—**Mike McGill**, all over it

… SSD IN PUSZONE … SWEEPER 5-0; YEAH? YOU TRY IT … TALES OF TERROR GET MENTAL … SKATING IS WHERE YOU MAKE IT: CHURCH PARKING LOT OR FUNERAL HOME OR VON'S … THE PHELPER MAKES PHOTO-G

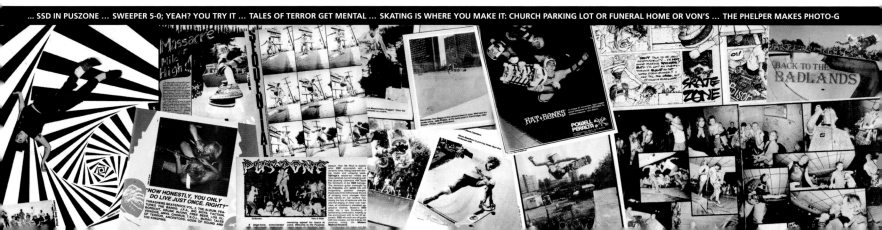

1985

"I'll see you in Disneyland."
—*Richard Ramierez*

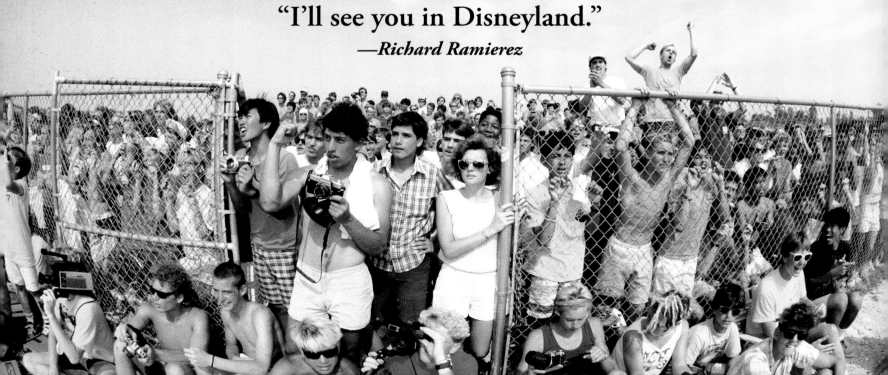

JEFF PHILLIPS
FRONTSIDE BONELESS / MOFO

NEIL BLENDER AND **A FRIEND**
MOFO

BILLY RUFF AND **NEIL BLENDER**
NO-COMPLY, ROLL BY / MOFO

CHRISTIAN HOSOI
ANDRECHT / MOFO

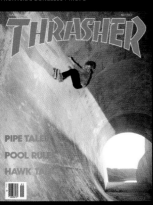

JOHN GIBSON
FRONTSIDE THRUST / THATCHER

STEVE CABALLERO
FRONTSIDE INVERT / MOFO

CHRIS MILLER
FRONTSIDE AIR / MOFO

LESTER KASAI
BACKSIDE AIR / MOFO

LANCE MOUNTAIN
PORTRAIT / MOFO

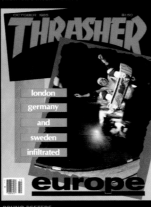

BRUNO PEETERS
FAKIE OLLIE / MOFO

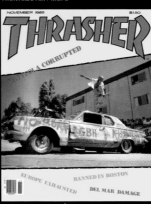

CHRISTIAN HOSOI
HEAD-HIGH FLY OVER / TKACHEFF

DAVE HACKETT
WALKOVER / VALESKA

1985

THE MAKING OF a skate video is well documented by masters Peralta and Stecyk. Steve Douglas, Bod Boyle, Sean Goff and others head up an able-bodied crew from the London region. Danny Webster, Martin Van Doren, Robby Butner, and Nicky Guerrero are also mentioned. Rodney and Caballero are in Japan with Toyoda and Rastaman. Dork sessions in Dallas are the rage. The Blue Ramp takes the brunt of the abuse. NSA invited the world's best to Huntington Beach for a pro/am skate-off. Motörhead is still a driving force from the blast box. Mark Gonzales arrives on the street style scene. Neil Blender claims back-to-back covers: only time ever. A lock at Lance's becomes a reality. VA Beach sets new standards in public ramp facilities. Joachim (Yo-Yo) Schultz of West Germany introduces the Yo-Yo plant. *Thrasher* gets color on the inside. Mofo's classic Whadda Bow Dem Niners piece is literary. Christian Hosoi talks about Madonna and Prince. Everybody is stoked on snowboarding. Frat rats throw down in the Thrash-a-Thon at Cal Poly. The number of skateparks with cement transitions is down to four. Texas pipes are re-awakened for big sessions. Pools rule. Cab's hair is tied and soldered for the June cover session. Ninety-degree transitions are negotiated regularly by Jesse Martinez and the boyz. Mile High madness continues with an NSA contest. VA Beach also gets into the act. Cycloid ramp theories are being developed. Mofo and a host of skate talent are turned loose on European shores. The famous "Butt Shots" article is a big hit with the conservative set. Madonna marries Sean Penn. Capitola is corrupted for the last time. Christ tops the field at NSA in Del Mar. Boston and New York City are terrorized.

Right: **Jeff Phillips** was a no-bullshit dude. High on acid, he whooped Hawk at the '86 NSA finals. Alley-oop frontside ollie at Lance's. On Christmas day 1993 he blew his brains out. Fuck

San Francisco had very few vert ramps; Sam Finger's in Hunters Point was the best. Visitor **Billy Ruff** liens one while **Olson** looks towards Castro Street

Mondo backside hip slip; you try it

Custom griptape jobs are rare now, but back in the day boards could last a month.
Holmes laps one into the channel at Lopes' ramp

Lance tore Del Mar. Check the front foot extension...
the word "proper" applied

LEGEND:
STEVE CABALLERO

By BILLY RUFF

"PREPARED." That's what I think of when the name Steve Caballero comes to mind. A couple years back—or make those decades—I had yet to meet Steve, but his reputation far preceded him. He was this kid from San Jose, CA, who would become the most unlikely skate champion. Put Steve in a room with 10 people and if you didn't know you would never expect him to become one of the most respected and innovative riders of his time.

To many people it was "Stevie," most likely due to his diminutive stature. But don't let that fool you. He was the guy that would stay up all night drawing out his competition lines, visualizing the skate venue, and playing out his routine in his mind. Everyone else would be out partying in the halls. Don't get me wrong, Steve was in the halls too, but work came first.

Steve and I spent a couple years going back and forth at many contests. Sometimes he'd win, sometimes I would, and of course there were a ton of other great skaters at the time to worry about as well. Usually Steve was the guy I set my watch by. Steve still skates to this day, and has collaborated on many products, including the world's top-selling skate shoe. When I see Steve in the skate mags these days it often brings me back to when we all skated for fun and the $250 first-place prize money. Good times.

"HIS REPUTATION FAR PRECEDED HIM"

The crowd may have been chanting "Twist! Twist Twist!" but **Cab** had yet to learn 'em—so he went ballistic. Mute so loud it hurts

OMER

MOFO

Johnee Kopp had the first handrail ad-photo in the mag, and lived up to the rep by blasting the car at Capitola

MOFO

Oh, you skate? How's 20 years of Harrison street? **Natas**, south-bound tailslide

Only **Lester** could sport his own shirt. The "Splash" graphics say it all: Meatballs don't bounce. High noon at Del Mar

SACTO STREET CONTEST—GONZ AND TG BOTH TURN PRO ... ANARCHY IN THE PARKING LOT ... HOSOI BLOWS OUT DEL MAR & SELLS BOARDS OUT OF HIS TRUNK ... JESS THE MESS, V13 FOR LIFE ...

Backyards: Where skating went underground

Holmes goes Rambo

No matter the terrain, **Mark Gonzales** would mimic vert wizardry. When there was no more tranny, the world followed suit

Lance joined the Bones Boys in '83, and by 1985 he was Top Gun. Burning down the round end of a square peg

"HE MADE IT POSSIBLE TO BE MYSTERIOUS"

LEGEND: NEIL BLENDER

By MARK GONZALES

I AM WRITING TO YOU IN HASTE. I got on the phone with Neil Blender in the early '80s. I spoke with him about who he skateboarded with. This is before street skating was a set event. He skated with Bob Serafin. "What sort of shit do you guys do?" I asked, and he said, "Rock and roll slide-in rolls in a roll." I was set to meet them and skate, but a car's capabilities to go from Hollywood, CA, to Fountain Valley, CA, made this not possible.

From photos that I saw of him in the mag, Neil's dress style made me ambitious; plaid flannel shirts with the arms cut off way up by the shoulders, army pants beneath his kneepads, and his helmet had a sticker of Dick Tracy. I thought that was funny, because his facial features were very similar. From his dress code to his skating style, he had an influence from people with a strong desire to make an impression but at the same time made it possible to be mysterious. I saw him riding halfpipe in Pomona, CA, and there was no flatbottom. I was watching from the fence and it looked like animals playing.

Billy Ruff was a personal favorite of mine. I don't care how homosexual that sounds. He would pop out six feet and kick his tail way out over the lip. That was cool. What Blender did was grab behind the foot and push the nose over the lip, forced and dorky like it was the opposite of what was cool. But both *were* cool. I think the Jolly Mamba is his best maneuver. I was included in a skate session that they were having at Skillman's ramp in Westminster, CA, and Blender did the smoothest boardslide to fakie to bu-bump. The sound of both sets of wheels popping off the oversized coping made you want to break someone's eardrums. How lovely it was, the Woolly Mammoth. I mean, the next time I skated with him was after a CASL event at Montrose, CA. He, John Lucero, and I were skating. Grosso was there too. Blender set up a way to boardslide the bleachers, starting off at a small point and dropping off the larger end. It was the start of a makeshift arrangement.

I always wanted to see him fight, but I never did. He got close to fighting me once and threw a kneepad at me. His anger was good, and luckily he harnessed it in a direction for all skateboarders to benefit from. Until our next duel, I'm signing off.

In the land of the 700 Club, this is about as close to God as you can get. **Blender**, frontal invert (note the front-foot accent and the cut-off socks used for elbow pad gaskets)

While **Frank Hawk** watches, **Grosso** gets sadder than a funeral

Heroes need fans

Hosoi was only 17 years old, and he could do anything he wanted

Opposite page: East Coast vert was loud, snotty, and obnoxious. **Freddy Smith** and the boys learned from the best and were more than happy to tell you about it. Think this qualifies as a "tuck-knee flappa." Nice chain, **Wrecka**

... HACKETT DROPS ACID ... THE NIGHT STALKER RULES CALIFORNIA ... BUTT SHOTS KILL AD REVENUE ... EDDIE REATEGUI JUMPS OFF THE ROOF AND INTO HP ... HR DESTROYS BABYLON ... TAHOE GETS FLAME-BROILED

1986

"Who'd I do this for, me or you?"

—*Glenn Danzig*

CLAUS GRABKE
INVERT / ROUSE

ALLEN LOSI
PORTRAIT, INVERT / MOFO

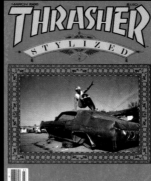

NATAS KAUPAS
BERT / BABOOT

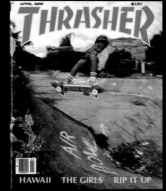

HAWAII   THE GIRLS   RIP IT UP

TOMMY GUERRERO
LIEN AIR / THATCHER

LESTER KASAI
FRONTSIDE OLLIE / MOFO

DANZIG

GLENN DANZIG
PORTRAIT / BURNS

JESSE MARTINEZ
JUDO / KEENAN

METALLICA

MIKE VALLELY SAD PLANT / MOFO
INSET: **JAMES HETFIELD** OF METALLICA / MOFO

ST. LOUIS
OUT OF CONTROL
SKATE ROCK
MUSICAL MAYHEM AT THE FARM
MARK GONZALES
OCEANSIDE STYLING

MARK GONZALES
BEANPLANT / MOFO

VACANCY
TRIX YOU
CAN'T DO
VENICE
SUMMER
STREET MEAT

TONY HAWK
FRONTSIDE GRIND / MOFO

"A NEW DISTRO
DEAL WITH KABLE
NEWS FORCED US
TO CHANGE THE
MAG SCHEDULE."
—*ED RIGGINS*

ROBBING
BANKS
FOR THOSE
INCLINED
ROB
ROSKOPP
INTERVIEW
VANCOUVER
INTERNATIONAL
SKATE EXPO

CHRIS MILLER
FRONTSIDE AIR / MOFO

1986

CULTURE CLASH. East meets West. Claus and Shane Rouse drop into Czechoslovakia. Massive terrain is on our minds. Puszone is happening. The art of downhill is not lost. Allen Losi eyes himself on the cover. *Thrasher* celebrates a five-year anniversary, and Natas gets so fired up he skates on the roof of a car. Freestyle fanatics refine it to an art form. Longboarding is given a short look. The pups of Dogtown—Oster, Murray, Dressen, Jackson, Martinez et al—carry on a longstanding tradition. Our poetic center spread raises eyebrows. KT clicks Tommy Guerrero for the cover of a Hawaii spread. The Fresno ark is huge. Girl skaters are given their due: B Blouin, Karen Zapata, Stephanie Person, April Hoffman, Michelle Sanderson are the sugar and spice. *Thrashin'*, the movie, is released and buried. Skateboarding is all over TV, billboards, at the movies, and in the mags more than ever. Cedar Crest Country Club is the choice ramp around…and it's not on the West Coast. Wallrides are going beyond vert. Blood, sweat, and tears fly at the Sacto street events. Ffej perfects the gymnast plant. Metallica is full-steam ahead and on everybody's Walkman. Gator is arrested at the VA Beach pro event. Keith Haring draws on a few skateboards; graphics are selling. Mullen's rep includes ollie airwalks, one-footed ollies, and 50-50 finger flip grab Melvins. Beastie Boys are pumping. St Louis is out of control while Gonzales gets an interview. We also talk to Rob Roskopp. Banks are robbed and Vision comes out with the first skate shoe in a while.

Maybe your dad built you a jump ramp. Rocket, Judo, Frigid, fingerflip; you may have had some skills, but fuck all that. Jukes are about blasting. Check **Holmes**' face: "Fuckin' **Gonz**…"

Opposite page: When **Grossman** was at this time in his life, baby, it was on. Hottest graphics, huge airs, bailed on the Bones Brigade… Ask him. Method at the 'Mar

Right: **TG**, skate rat

OMER

THATCHER

LEGEND:
CHRIS MILLER

By CHRISTIAN HOSOI

CHRIS MILLER WAS NOT only one of the most influential skaters of all time, but he was also one of the most influential skaters in my life because of his speed, style, and grace. I remember Chris being very mellow when it came to hanging out, but as soon as he got on his board he was all business. And it hasn't changed. I believe Chris is a big part of why skateboarding still has some integrity when it comes to reputation. He represents a personality that I can look up to not only as a skater, but also as a person. He's a great husband, father, and businessman.

Chris is still at the top of his game today. He came out of nowhere and took the Vans-Protec combi-bowl contest, and I just saw him at the X Games busting 14-foot frontside airs on Danny Way's Mega Ramp. He is still ruling it. Yeah Miller! One thing I like about him the most is that he makes skateboarding look so easy, fluid, and stylish.

Let's not explain it like "wow," "rad," or "kill." How about: "beautiful." **Miller** in Vancouver with a lien torque, and a Houston backside boner

"HE MAKES SKATEBOARDING LOOK SO EASY, FLUID, AND STYLISH"

Frank Hawk ruled behind the fence, but on the other side he caught a lot of shit

Gator snaps one at a ditch in SD. The hat, torn-up jeans—this is skateboarding

Wallos in Hawaii is no Christmas party. Rough and kinked, it's a great place to lose some skin or break some legs. **Cab** early-grabs frontside while filming the *Animal Chin* opener

Fingers Murray lays one down at Oceanside. Real street, vert judges, and **Terrence Yoshizawa**

DUDE, THIS AIR OF HOLMES DOING A ROCKET WAS TOO INSANE. YOU TRY IT, FOOL … CAB GOES 10-FEET … D BOON DIES, SAN PEDRO WEEPS … JOHNEE KOPP HAS THE FIRST HANDRAIL AD (CAVEMAN) … BARREL JUMP? …

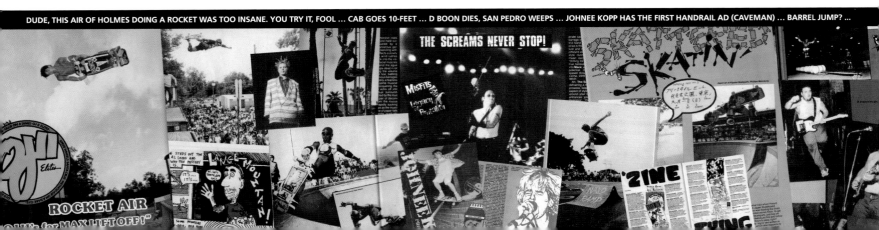

MOFO

In every boom box next to every ramp—everywhere—
it's **Metallica** to hype the sesh. **Hetfield**, creeping death

... 'ZINE THING IS ON ... METALLICA RULES, CLIFF BURTON DIES ...

The late Cliff Burton, Cow Palace, S.F., June 1986.

NoTes

Above: Underrated and elusive, **Tom Groholski** was one of the first pros from the East Coast. His dad shot his cover photo at the ramp in their backyard. This ollie to grind over a metal monster in Houston is downright barbaric

... THROW ANOTHER ON THE FIRE ... MARK GONZALES GETS INTERVIEWED AND HIS SHIRT SAYS "BRAINWASH VICTIM" ... TERROR RAINS ... THE CROMAGS RIP, GLENN DANZIG IS STILL SMALL ... GONZO GETS INVERTED BRO

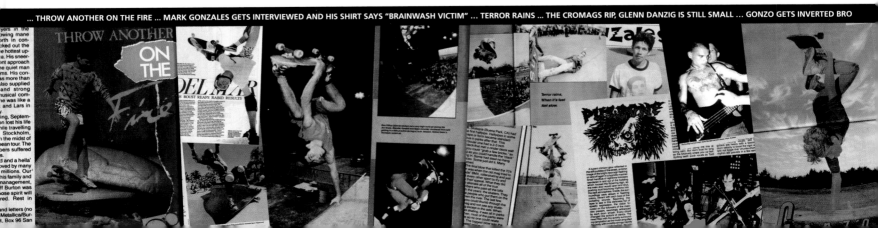

PUSHEAD

I'VE KNOWN PUSHEAD for about 25 years now. We both lived in Boise, ID, prior to transplanting to SF, CA. We'd been making frequent skate trips and tours with his band Septic Death, hanging out with Tim Yohannon (RIP) and Jeff Bale in the early Maximum Rock'n'Roll days, or going to the mag ("Puszone") and to record and bookstores to get our fixes. I also attribute our journeys together with eventually landing me my job at *Thrasher*. Pus turned me onto a lot of cool stuff and I've met a priceless shit pot of friends and associates along the way; in fact, the most interesting, dedicated, and down-to-earth people I know.

"MANY PAINSTAKING AND CRYPTICALLY METHODICAL PIECES"

Pus was a major influence and developer in both our punk and skate scenes in Boise. He promoted shows, encouraged others to get involved, and built ramps. Later he took DIY to the next level and started his own record labels—Pusmort and Bacteria Sour—produced albums, wrote articles and music reviews for magazines, and even created his own clothing and toy lines. His resume of accomplishments and contributions is endless.

One of Pushead's starting points was drawing album covers for bands like Wasted Youth, the FU's, and SSD to name a few; although, he became more of a household name for his work with Metallica as well as his now infamous board graphics for Zorlac skateboards. Deserving and finally achieving recognition by the art world in recent years, I've witnessed many painstaking and cryptically methodical pieces, while observing his style continually develop (he's a master of stippling). It's pretty amazing the concentrated effort he puts into each and every endeavor. I understand why so many have and continue to seek his artwork for their bands and album cover art. Search eBay for a hint of the value his work holds today.

Always straight-forward and opinionated, Pushead still remains humble, on top of things, and continues to amaze the art, music, and skateboarding communities. Pushead is true—to the flesh and bone—to his friends, fans, and critics. —*Rick Rotsaert*

1987

"Hot. Reckless. Totally insane."
—Thrashin' *movie ad*

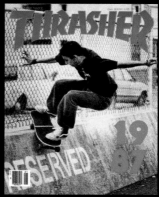

JIM THIEBAUD
FRONTSIDE GRIND / MOFO

CHRIS DOHERTY
GANG GREEN / MOFO

1986 PRO-AM CLIMAX
ADOLESCENTS
TWO CITIES
—THE GAME

JEFF PHILLIPS
FRONTSIDE OLLIE / MOFO

TALL TALES

BRIAN BRANNON
BACKSIDE KICKTURN / KANIGHTS

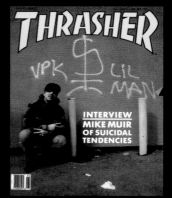

INTERVIEW
MIKE MUIR
OF SUICIDAL
TENDENCIES

MIKE MUIR
PORTRAIT / MOFO

SUMMER
BUST
OUT
ISSUE

STEVE ALBA
CARVE / KEENAN

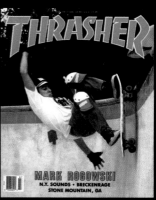

MARK ROGOWSKI
N.Y. SOUNDS • BRECKENRAGE
STONE MOUNTAIN, GA

MARK ROGOWSKI
SLASHBACK / MOFO

TONY HAWK
FRONTSIDE OLLIE / THATCHER

GOD'S
LAND
OF BITCHES
HOT
AMS
SOME OF THE BEST
TORONTO
A GREAT SHOW

"FIRE PICK"
ARTWORK BY PUSHEAD

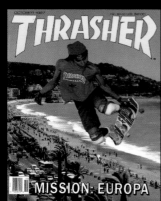

MISSION: EUROPA

CHRISTIAN HOSOI
METHOD AIR / MOFO

POOL
JONES

SUPER RAMP
The Rise and The Fall

MISSION:
EUROPA Part II

STEVE CABALLERO
FRONTSIDE BOARDSLIDE / MOFO

SLAMMIN'
STREETSTYLE IN
SAVANNAH
TAHITI
ADVENTURE
IN PARADISE
BAILS
THE FALL GUY'S
DICTIONARY
D.R.I.
DECENT
RIGHTEOUS
INDIVIDUALS!

EDDIE REATEGUI
FRONTSIDE THRUSTER / KEENAN

1987

THE '86 PRO SEASON winds down with the Chicago Blowout. Hawk first, Cab second, Hosoi third. Meanwhile, over in Europe, Pierre Andre, Gunter Molokuys, Frank Messman and Gogo Sprieter are ripping. Street style goes back to Eugene, OR, and gets rained on again. Pushead tells of large metal pipes out Boise way. Anthrax wears high tops and jams. Skatemaster Tate and the Sirens work LA. Gang Green hits hard on our first rock cover. NSA goes to Arizona where it's Hawk, followed by Hosoi and Caballero. Lance Benson is one ripping skate rat. The sound that roars in '87 is Samhain, Jesus and Mary Chain, COC, DRI, Accused, Butthole Surfers, Big Black, Sonic Youth, etc. Nosepicks are now a skate maneuver. Hawk misses a McTwist at the NSA finals in Anaheim and Jeff Philips walks away with first place buckage. Reese Simpson takes am honors. Christian soars to 10 1/2 over. Atari announces the 720 video game. Brannon's Tall Tales spin yards of yarn. Suicidal Mike Muir talks. Happening ramps include Page Mill, Chris Robison's and Cambodia. Rocco's Hell Tour chronicles life on the road. Spuds Mackenzie rides a board on TV. A posse of pros demos Dayton while a skate rock party ensues in Austin, TX. Upland Pipeline celebrates 10 glorious years. NSA goes to Stone Mountain, GA. Gator is nabbed for an overdue interview. Snowboarding goes worldly at Breckenridge. Street plants are dying on the vine. The Big Apple sound is loud and hard. Douglass and Bod are on the run in the USA. KT follows the pro tour to Oz. East Coasters boast a heavy metal ramp scene. Megadeath moshes. Pros hit Toronto. El Gato is back. Mo goes Mission Europa. Great Britain bites back. Hell ramp teeters. NSA goes back to St Looey. We go back to Willamette, dammit. Am Bams include Marlowe, Mank, Tocco, Byrd, Spalero, Castro, Fabriquer, Froland, Istavanick, Boettcher, and others.

Jesse "The Mess" Martinez was so close to getting a board on Powell, and… Let's just say he didn't take no shit at Disneyland. V13 in your face—he'd break three boards before noon everyday

Opposite page: This spot in Paris looked like Skate Heaven, but the bricks kinda sucked. **Shorty** creaks a crap on Bastille Day

NATAS OLLIES UP AND OVER A CAR … RAGING WATERS & CHRISTIAN COMBINE FOR A WHOPPER 540 … ANIMAL CHIN? NEVER HEARD OF IT … BLACKHART RACING CARS? … NATAS' HYDRANT SPIN IS OUT OF THIS WORLD …

He's in prison now, but **Gator** could spin a mean five. St Louis feels the noise

"YOU BETTER HAVE A CAMERA"

When you look this good you better have a camera

Left: Raging Waters water park, vert mega-monster, and **Jason Jessee** before tats. Disposable hero? Fuck no

The shot heard 'round the word: The **Gonz** jumping The Gonz. And…your name is what?

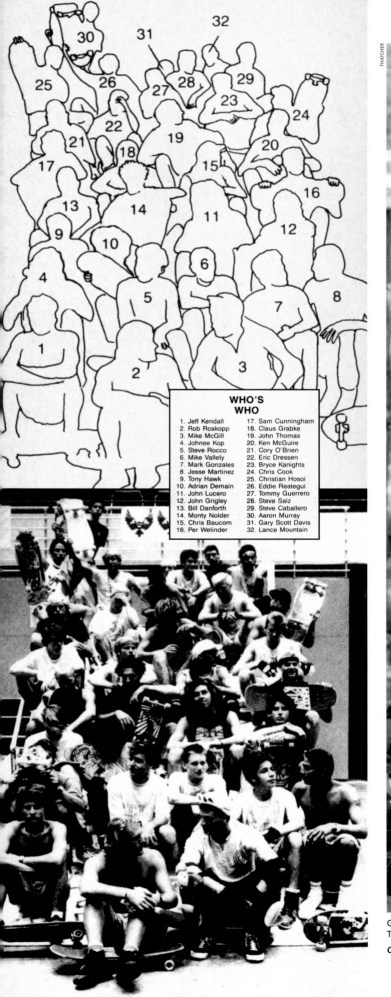

WHO'S WHO

1. Jeff Kendall
2. Rob Roskopp
3. Mike McGill
4. Johnee Kop
5. Steve Rocco
6. Mike Vallely
7. Mark Gonzales
8. Jesse Martinez
9. Tony Hawk
10. Adrian Demain
11. John Lucero
12. John Grigley
13. Bill Danforth
14. Monty Nolder
15. Chris Baucom
16. Per Welinder
17. Sam Cunningham
18. Claus Grabke
19. John Thomas
20. Ken McGuire
21. Cory O'Brien
22. Eric Dressen
23. Bryce Kanights
24. Chris Cook
25. Christian Hosoi
26. Eddie Reategui
27. Tommy Guerrero
28. Steve Saiz
29. Steve Caballero
30. Aaron Murray
31. Gary Scott Davis
32. Lance Mountain

THATCHER

Gold Cup Andrecht by **Neil Blender**. Such a gnarly trick on lots of vert. That's why they call them legends. Houston

Opposite page: **Natas**, 10-stair boardslide in 1987! Think about it, dinglenuts

LEGEND:
TOMMY GUERRERO

By MIKE VALLELY

IT DOESN'T GET ANY HEAVIER than Tommy Guerrero. In the thick of the mid '80s, TG rose up and put it down like no one else before or since. We're talking pure streetstyle, the real deal. Not walking back from the rail to turn around to hit it again and again, but ever flowing, adapting, and creating on the spot and in the moment. He moved through The City and redefined every inch of it. This isn't the type of shit you can just capture on Beta cam. You have to fucking live it; words and frozen images only tell an inkling of the story. The rest you only know and understand when you put your board down and hit the streets. It's future fucking primitive. This was the birth of street skating and TG was there. The revolution lived inside him.

Left: Hell Hole is called so because it's in Colma, CA, where there are more dead people than live ones. **Tommy G** was all up in that shit

Right: To be honest, I bet Tommy still thinks about the back and ankles when he sees this shot

"WE'RE TALKING PURE STREETSTYLE THE REAL DEAL"

MOTÖRHEAD

THE MAG AND MOTÖRHEAD go hand in hand, and, like good wine, get better when aged.

TOP 10 SONGS FOR ANY ROAD TRIP:

♠ "Hoochie Coochie Man"

♠ "Love Me Like A Reptile"

♠ "Dead Men Tell No Tales"

♠ "Fast and Loose"

♠ "Overkill"

♠ "On Parole"

♠ "Beer Drinkers & Hell Raisers"

♠ "Rock 'N' Roll"

♠ "Built for Speed"

♠ "Iron Horse/Born to Lose"

Finding a spot and doing something scary is all **Gonzo** territory. SLO-Town; this shit was hard—look at his face

... *THRASHIN'* THE MOVIE? ... POWELL GIVES THE FIRST GIRLS AN AD ... HOLMES GOES 10+ AT THE VISION SKATE ESCAPE ... ROSKOPP HAD THE BEST THRUSTER ... MURRAY, HOSOI, AND OSTER SKATE TUFF ON ROCKETS

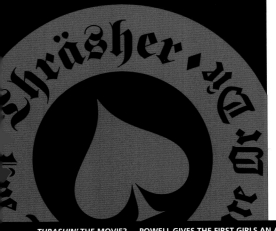

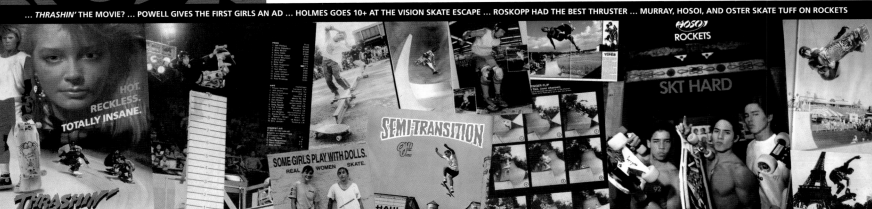

1988

"I'm the worst skater ever."

—*Neil Blender*

THRASHER

THE OLDEST TRICKS ARE NOT WHAT YOU THINK

CONTESTS: TAKE IT OR LEAVE IT

DEE DEE RAMONE MOUTHS OFF

EAST COAST AMS

PHOTOGRAFFITI

ERIC DRESSEN
TAIL TAP / KATZ

THRASHER

SKATER: TONY VITELLO
MODEL: KATRINA BAUMGARTNER / STECYK

THRASHER

FIASCO IN ARIZONA
THE N.S.A. EXPOSED

TOMMY GUERRERO
DEFINES GRAVITY

SCOTT OSTER
SQUATTED G-TURN / KATZ

THRASHER

GO FIND YOUR OWN SPOT
Stop Whining Stop Looking

COJONES
Do You Have What It...

WORLD'S GREATEST SKATER

STEVE ALBA
FRONTSIDE TAP-IN / KEENAN

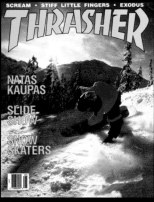

THRASHER

NATAS KAUPAS

SLIDE SHOW

SNOW SKATERS

ROB ROSKOPP
SNOWDOG / KANIGHTS

THRASHER

Skatetown Chronicles

Double Trouble

Mini-Ramp Challenge

Damage in Dayton

CHRISTIAN HOSOI
FAKIE OLLIE / BLANCHARD

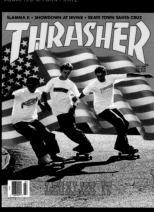

THRASHER

LEGALIZE IT

JOHN DETTMAN, DANNY SARGENT,
& LUKE OGDEN HAIRPIN TURN / KANIGHTS

THRASHER

INTERVIEW
ERIC DRESSEN

extraordinary
ROBERT WILLIAMS

"MAKE YOUR OBSESSION PALATABLE…"
ARTWORK BY ROBERT WILLIAMS

THRASHER

ALIENS INVADE TORONTO

Phoenix, AZ denizens unearth bizarre terrain — Wild youths actually skate it!

WORLD EXCLUSIVE
SKATERS BEHIND BARS

SAM ESMOER
FLOATER / MOFO

THRASHER

TERRAIN FOR THE INSANE

¿QUE PASA IN ALBUQUERQUE?

BATTERED MAN RETURNS

RIGGED, RIPPED AND DAMAGED

DAVID HACKETT
FRONTSIDE GRIND / KATZ

THRASHER

JAKS

METRO D.C. REPORT

PINBALL MANIA

BOD BOYLE
BACK LIP / KANIGHTS

THRASHER

BIG NAMES ON LITTLE RAMPS

TRUE CONFESSIONS
I Ollied The Berlin Wall

BOISE MEMOIRS

EAT LUNCHMEAT

LANCE MOUNTAIN
SAD PLANT / OGDEN

1988

WE LOOK AT the over-30-and-still-rolling set. Raging Waters holds an air show featuring Caballero and 10-feet over, while the NSA finds an empty velodrome for free and street. Duane Peters re-enters the limelight. Lip tricks are being exploited to the fullest. Hot shoes on the East Coast: Mike Conroy, Rob Mertz, Mike Crescini, Dan Brown, Sergie Ventura, Dave Lemieuz, and Clint Deaton. Dee Dee Ramone is still wearing high tops. Eastern Eden includes the Farm ramp, Cedar Crest, Cambridge pool, and Ocean Bowl ramp. Freddy Kreuger terrorizes the mag. A chlorine dust storm swirls around the NSA event at Big Surf in Tempe, Arizona. Tommy Guerrero talks. Skate bands abound: Odd Man Out, Ungh!, Ghoul Squad, Hell's Kitchen, Token Entry, and McRad to name a few. Salba and cohorts hightail it to English shores. Joey McSqueeb makes his debut. Bill Tocco is am champion. Other rippers: Dave Nielson, John Fudala, Troy Chasen, Gene Hare, and Brian Pennington. Skaters are scuffing walls all over the country. Surf 'N' Turf reopens to rave reviews. Natas is revealed in words and more pictures. Mount Baker snowboard event is chillin'. Stiff Little Fingers is back. Skatetown Sacto is revisited. Savannah gets slammed again. Tony can't win the big ones as Christian takes down 5,000 clams at the NSA finals in Irvine. Eric Dressen doubles up with Robert Williams for a big interview issue. Curbs are cool again. Aliens invade Toronto. Dedders escapes from Alcatraz. Phoenix is follied. Potato Head says, "Plan your skate day." Zodiac warps minds. Kentucky gets fried. Albuquerque is checked and the terrain is insane. Jaks team goes on a roll in Santa Barbara. Münster is a monster for Mofo. Sacto mini-ramp is a burner. Berlin and Boise are in the same issue. So are Social Distortion and Guns 'N' Roses.

Eric Dressen, signature salad

SKATERS DOING UP THEIR OWN GRAPHICS BECOMES THE NORM ... COLIN MCKAY GETS HIS FIRST PHOTO IN THE MAG ... JULIEN STRANGER FRONT BOARDS EVERETT ... RAGING WATERS GOES *GUINNESS BOOK* ...

OMER

"LIP TRICKS ARE BEING EXPLOITED TO THE FULLEST"

MOFO

THRASH

Danny Way, age 13

Jason Jessee, Christ air

MARK GONZALES & ALCATRAZ: USE A SKATE, GO TO PRISON ... ARC BACK SMITHS THE HUNTERS POINT RAMP ... COMICS ... LEE RALPH HAS A LAUGH ...

USE A SKATE GO TO PRISON

BATTERED MAN

perverse!

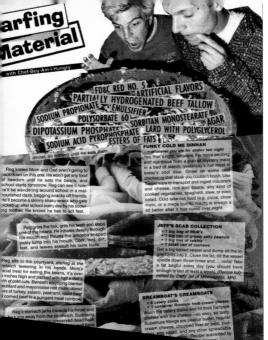

SKARFING MATERIAL

THE MALICE of Mary's Surprise? Maggot Farouche? Skaters are a hungry lot, and adventurous at that—so leave it to *Thrasher* to come up with Skarfing Material, a colorful concoction of culinary… well, in most cases, crap. Calorie and carb counts be damned; we're talking a monthly column that started with a little fiction and ended with reader-submitted recipes built of ingredients like desiccated brussel sprouts, dried toad skins, green velvet bean bags (green peppers), and a sliced large fungus…amongst other less-healthful morsels.

The plans for Pip San's Chili-Shroom appetizers, for instance:

♠ A large Ziploc bag of killer mushrooms
♠ One can of your favorite chili
♠ Several slices of cheese

Wash the 'shrooms, then pull out their stumps. Hollow the insides until you have what resembles a small, drained pool. Now pack each vessel with chili and nuke 'em 'til they bubble. Remove and groove, cat.
—*Ryan Henry*

Venice/Dogtown since the beginning of time; **Tim Jackson** at Ground Zero

Opposite page: **Gator**'s lines were way beyondo: first-hit Miller flips to every trick in the book. He won a couple but was overlooked for not going as high… Still, this backside ollie shows his mastership of the stuntwood

… KEVIN STABB GROWS HIS HAIR AND HANGS OUT WITH THE CULT … PUBLIC ENEMY ARE IN, RAP IS COOL … SONIC YOUTH ROCKS & ROLLS … ROCCO? THE PHOTO SAYS IT ALL …

When **Tony Hawk** finally left this wonder-structure in Fallbrook, he wished he could have "lit it on fire."
How prophetic. This frontside is burning in North County

Opposite page: **Steve Claar** Madonna

The Torquay ramp was the spot for **Hosoi**
to demonstrate "proper" skating. Check the
background: **Ralph**, **Ellis**, **Crescini**, and the very
elusive **Gregor Rankin**

Brian Ferdinand slappies a tough spot that came
and went as quickly as he did

Frontside torque-on

LEGEND:
THE
GONZ

By CAIRO FOSTER

TODAY IS NEITHER the beginning nor the end of skateboarding. Mark Gonzales did not create skateboarding, and he will not end skateboarding. He has been doing the same thing each and every skater has been doing his or her whole life as a skateboarder: skateboarding. However, it's the rest of us that restrain ourselves from reaching our full potential. But, when someone disregards the barriers that define the norm, they surpass "average" and risk the chance of being ostracized—possibly being pushed to the sidelines and overlooked. Fortunately for us, Mark has not been banished to the sidelines.

When it comes to skateboarding there will always be someone better. Are there people out there that can do more tricks than Mark? Yes. Is there someone better than the Gonz? No. But he's not defining what skateboarding should be. Keep in mind that a skateboard is just an inanimate object that Mark happened to pick up instead of some other thing. Mark is using a skateboard to outline how we should live our lives—no boundaries.

Monkey + Einstein + Bob Dylan = **Mark Gonzales**

"HOW WE SHOULD LIVE OUR LIVES— NO BOUNDARIES"

Rad mag madman **Lee Ralph** came to play

He did 80 ollies in a row on this ramp and cleared 11 feet. **Holmes**

Take a number and sit down—Seattle board check

OG Kenter crew

1989

"Salba, we were here,
you weren't."
—*Zipperhead*

THRASHER

1989 skateboarding is . . .

JAY ADAMS
GRIND / HUDSON

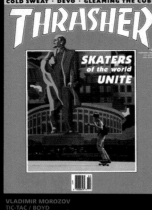

THRASHER

SKATERS of the world UNITE

VLADIMIR MOROZOV
TIC-TAC / BOYD

THRASHER

CAN YOU . . .
KEEP UP WITH RODNEY?
SURF A GREAT LAKE?
SKATEABOUT AUSTRALIA?
. . . YEAH YOU CAN

ROBBY OLHISER
WALLRIDE / STARR

THRASHER

lust for life

BRIAN BRANNON
FAKIE THRUST / THATCHER

THRASHER

SEVEN SEQUEN
STEE
BACKYARDS B
ITALIAN STY
SKATER AN
THE GHOST
LIVING COLO
CHRIS MILLER
NSA FINALS
KILLER POOL
THE MINI-EST R
SKATERS VERSUS
THE PEDESTRIAN
TWOFOURSEVEN
POOLS-A-PLEN
STAR TREK

CHRIS MILLER
PORTRAIT / MOFO

THRASHER

COLLECTOR'S EDITION

History of the Skateboard

ISSUE 100

interviews:
PETERS
HOSOI
CABALLERO
HAWK

JOHN HUTSON
AT SPEED / CASSELLI

THRASHER

San Francisco

The steepest
loudest
meanest
fastest
weirdest
gnarliest
coolest
punkest
skatetown
on the whole
damn planet.

RON ALLEN
FRONTSIDE BOARDSLIDE / KANIGHTS

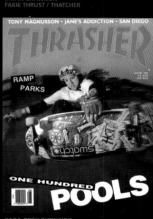

THRASHER

RAMP PARKS

ONE HUNDRED POOLS

CARA-BETH BURNSIDE
FRONTSIDE AIR / CAVALHEIRO

THRASHER

BRAIN BOMB
EXPLOSIVE PHOTOS

GLOBAL INVASION
GET OUTTA TOWN

AERIAL SEARCH

DANNY SARGENT
NOSEPICK / THATCHER

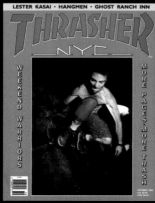

THRASHER
NYC

WEEKEND WARRIORS

MORE PAGES MORE TRASH

JEREMY HENDERSON
WALLRIDE / THOMAS

THRASHER

So-realist MANIACS turn art upside down

BAD BRAINS / RAW MEAT

SCOTT OSTER
BERT / VAN DUSEN

THRASHER

144 PAGES

LONDON CALLING

SNAKES and REPTILES

MÜNSTER MOSH

JEFF KENDALL

JEFF KENDALL
FRONTSIDE SMITH GRIND / OSCARSSON

1989

DANFORTH RINGS in the new year while Hackett tells it. Operation Ivy is alive and well. NSA goes to the fair in SF. Devo returns and the Sugarcubes are still a band. Christian Slater learns to turn from the Bones Brigade. *Thrasher* hits Russia—Vladimir Lenin makes the cover as skaters of the world unite. Deceased street plants go to hell. We turn over our 100th issue. Great Lakes get surfed, mountains get bombed. Rodney flows with freestyle philosophy. Skatetown: San Francisco, and two months later, The City gets hit by seismic waves. Pools from above. Slamma. Slayer. Pipeline dies, Chris Miller lives. Living Colour and 24-7 Spyz, Jane's Addiction, Bad Brains, Excel, zounds for days.

Stan the man and **Jean** his wife made skating their life. We owe, big time

Right: Badlands blade **Malba** groundhogs while Mothra **Grossman** liens over Chino. Check the shadow for props

THATCHER

Matt Hensley was every kid's fave skater. Tack-sharp and razor-clean schoolyard frontside

LEE RALPH IS NO NATE JONES … SLAYER BEFORE DAVE LOMBARDO RAN OUT OF GAS … KICKFLIP INDYS HAD NO LUCK INVOLVED … NATAS, TOMMY, AND JIMMY: HERMANOS …

In one of the H-Street vids, **John Sonner** claims "Vista is where it's at." For him, it sure was. Real method on a structure that saw some runs

"Sprung" is the only way to describe this totally random shot of **Harold Hunter** at Brooklyn Bridge Banks

Squeebs be damned, "Twist! Twist! Twist!"

The first skate shoe dude, **Natas Kaupas** wallies out of Louisville

Opposite page: Serious ollie merchant **Lester Kasai** ripped Sadlands like few others before they dozed it. FSO on a Lunar landscape

THE
PHELPER

JAKE PHELPS called me one night, inquiring about how things are going in his usual blunt, semi-rude-but-caring fashion. But this conversation was different than others; the quick-witted Phelps rambled on about a *Thrasher* book, some words like "vert is for girls," something about Burnside, and "199 in your prime." It was a little early to deal with, but later in the day I decided to use the power of the pen and write something.

"IF YOU ARE A RIDER, YOU WILL NEVER GROW OLD"

Skateboarding is the most fun there is. With the right tunes and people pumping it up, the whole deal is a working harmony feeling other people's power by creating the ultimate power-jam mega mix. I know I'm not alone when I say these times are priceless. Keep ripping, everyone. Crank up the tunes so loud you don't have to talk or listen to anyone—you can just ride.

A very special thanks and respect to Jake Phelps for all of his dedication to this deal and his job. Jake Phelps is *Thrasher*. You love him and hate him, but that's what makes him unique. Nevertheless, he's always been there. If you're a rider, you will never grow old. I will simply ride into eternity, skateboarding forever.
—*Mark "Red" Scott*

OGDEN

Team Pierre was still doing his shit wherever the hell he wanted. Epic dude, classic spot—Fort Miley

THATCHER

Known at first as the New Powell Kids, **Guy Mariano**, **Paulo Diaz**, **Rudy Johnson**, and **Gabriel Rodriguez** quickly scared all the vert pros into writing resumes and looking for real jobs

THOMAS

Red or blue, what's your set?

Allegedly not winning the big one because he didn't go as big as Hawk or Hosoi, **Gator** definitely had the deepest bag of tricks. Alley-oop saran wrap at Fallbrook, two years before porn and drugs caused his own personal Chernobyl

In his prime, **Holmes** was untouchable in any backyard situation. The story of this pool was straight religious. Flatspots and square cope at the end of a long, hot Arizona day

LEGEND:
DANNY WAY

By JOHN CARDIEL

INTEGRITY IS BEING GOOD when no one is around, and that is precisely what it takes to reach the heights of Danny Way's skating. He came up through the pro ranks as a force demanding respect from the veterans of the era. Blasting on the scene in Hawaii in 1989, a mini-ramp showdown exposed to the masses his arsenal of weaponry. Skateboarding would never be the same. Danny went on to sweat out some of the most ground breaking video parts, from the H-Street videos to Plan B to the present day DC video, which features some of the most balls-to-the-wall skating ever on the Mega Ramp he constructed. Danny's ability to excel in every aspect of skating is unparalleled, with 540s in pools, anaconda rails, backside noseblunt slides, and the highest airs ever. Check the deep files D Way has rolled away from, not to mention countless injuries like reconstructive surgeries with no anesthesia and a snapped neck. Danny has seen his fair share of battle.

If you ever have the chance to speak to Danny, you'll witness his intense energy and a skull-piercing glare that only warriors exude. While standing atop 100-foot scaffolding with reminiscence of loved ones and visuals of others, preparing to launch over the Great Wall of China, do you think there was any lack of confidence or second-guessing? I don't think so.

Hold it right there! Seen from the roof of the Hard Rock, **Danny** drops the bomb in Vegas. Too sick

"INTENSE ENERGY AND A
SKULL-PIERCING GLARE"

THATCHER

Danny goes his own way. Method at Knox in Oz

THATCHER

ORTIZ

Noah Peacock crails at an SF schoolyard

Lance flashes to tail on the love seat

... NATAS, STYLE EYES ... JANE'S ADDICTION AND TOM GROHOLSKI ARE BOTH RATED AS HOT ... POWELL GOES LEATHER ... GONZ JUMPS A CHANNEL IN HAWAII, PHILLIPS BONELESSED IT

1990

"Skateboarding is the
sound of living."

—*Jake Phelps*

STEVE CABALLERO
BONED INDY TO FAKIE / MOFO

GEORGE NAGAI FRONTSIDE AIR / STARR
INSET: MIKE RANQUET ROCKS OUT / MILLER

MARC HOLLANDER
CARVE / STARR

KARMA TSOCHEFF
MULTI STROBE / VAN DUSEN

FRANKIE HILL
RAILSLIDE / MOFO

BUTCH STERBINS
RAILSLIDE / MOFO

TIM GALVIN
PIPE THRUSTER / THATCHER

BOB PEREYRA
LUGE / KATZ

AARON DEETER
FRONTSIDE AIR / MOFO

BRENNAND SCHOEFFEL
OLLIE / KANIGHTS

HENRY SANCHEZ
BACKSIDE NOSEGRIND / THATCHER

OMAR HASSAN
LIEN AIR / STARR

1990

TATTOOS. Trash-a-thon. Should I skate or should I snow? Grosso is addicted. Ice T reps the mag and skateboarding gets its own TV show on Nickelodeon. Boston versus Tokyo versus Texas. Danny Way is still an upstart. *Hokus Pokus.* Faith No More followed by New Kids on the Block followed by the Buzzcocks? Survival Research Labs. Frankie Hill is the King of Santa Barbara. The Last Invert. New Orleans. Bart Simpson and Gwar. Polynesia. Street luge. Omar and Knox. Free pinball machines. The revolution begins: vert crosses street in a mini-ramp evolution. One month earlier, Sanchez makes the cover at EMB.

Samhain in Texas

Angel Santiago got the name Coco from his mom, who said that he looked like a coconut when he was born. On a board, he'd blow you into nothitude. Ask Bam. Early Palo Alto

Opposite page: **Henry Sanchez** was one of the first SF skaters to shock the street world. From Spitfire ads to Real, the kid was on hit. Bluntslide at Sears going Mach Five. Highway to hell

MARKOVICH ON RADAR FROM FLA ... GROSSO: "DRUGS ARE OUT" ... SANCHEZ BLASTS FOR THE FIRE ... BOREAL SNOW STYLE, CARS GET WRECKED ... DANNY WAY: DEVILISH GRIN OF THINGS TO COME ...

Hey, it's me . . .
JEFF GROSSO

S.O.T.Y.

SKATER OF THE YEAR is *Thrasher*'s award to the skateboarder who best represented our mag over the past 12 months. Some come out of the blue, and some have it nailed from the get-go. Here's to all the past and future SOTYs. —*Jake Phelps*

1990	Tony Hawk
1991	Danny Way
1992	John Cardiel
1993	Salman Agah
1994	Mike Carroll
1995	Chris Senn
1996	Eric Koston
1997	Bob Burnquist
1998	Andrew Reynolds
1999	Brian Anderson
2000	Geoff Rowley
2001	Arto Saari
2002	Tony Trujillo
2003	Mark Appleyard
2004	Danny Way
2005	Chris Cole

Sacto, in its prime, produced some of the gnarliest dudes. Curtis, Mess, Ross Goodman, Troy Miller, Cards, and this guy, **Snaggle**—totally beyond the realm of kindness. Long live Dirty Sac

Opposite page: Just when you thought he went away, **Gonz** shows up and says, "How about fuck off?"
Straight leg frontside from hip to extension

Mike Carroll lien grabs at 43, by the New Spot

Hosoi rolls into the sunset, and we sold over 1,000,000 painters caps

January contest at Boreal: **Cardiel** nosegrinds the car before the Sacto boys played wrecking ball. Templeton won it

... STRANGER LEAVES HOME BECAUSE OF HIS SYRINGE GRAPHICS ... MCGILL CALLS GUY & RUDY AND ASKS TO SKATE ... HENSLEY AND BARBEE ARE STREET PRINCES ... HOSOI DEMOS AT BLOOMINGDALES ... BLIND IS BORN

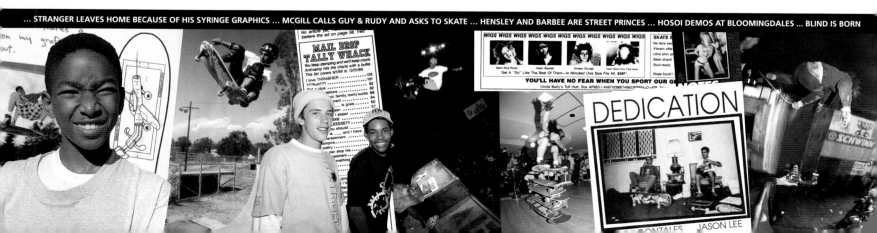

LEGEND:
TONY HAWK

By LESTER KASAI

IT WAS THE SUMMER OF 1980 and the Association of Skatepark Owners (ASPO) held an amateur contest at the Oasis skateboard park in San Diego, CA. My mother drove me down to Oasis the weekend before the contest so I could practice for the pool event. This was my third major amateur contest and my very first time visiting the Oasis skatepark.

Once I was in the park, I proceeded to the keyhole pool to practice. There was a very small and skinny blond-haired kid skating in the pool. To my amazement, this tiny 12-year-old kid was executing various ollies, varials, and shove-it tricks. At that period of time, I had never seen anyone do some of the tricks that he was performing. His innovation at such a young age was outstanding. I could tell that this kid was a gifted and unique individual. Tony Hawk was his name, and surprisingly he did not have an attitude problem like many young, talented skateboarders do today. I have always admired that quality about Tony. He was a nice guy and I became quite good friends with him after that day.

Despite Tony's first-class bag of tricks, there were individuals who would publicly ridicule Tony for his skating style during the '80s. These individuals would negatively comment on how he would ollie into all of his tricks. Consequently, they would believe that Tony's technique was not the politically correct way to ride a skateboard.

As time went on, those individuals who ridiculed Tony would realize that his style was necessary to accomplish the maneuvers that would bring skating to the next level and pave the way for modern vertical skateboarding. Tony's style was no longer ridiculed—but duplicated by the masses. Tony is by far the one reason why vertical skateboarding has reached such a high level of difficulty. In the end, it looks like Tony got the last laugh.

This photo of **Tony Hawk** is amazing. That's the square part of the combi; tuck-knee invert on Pringle can cope. This pool ate people for breakfast, but Tony's the only one to ever nail a 540 in the square

"DUPLICATED
BY THE
MASSES"

'ZINES ARE the people's choice. They slag, they suck, they rule, and they're homegrown fun. Get a Xerox machine, a stapler, think up a stupid name, and presto—you're famous

1991

"Last night, before I went to sleep,
I was thinking, 'Gay twist varial disasters'."

—*Tony Hawk*

TONY HAWK
MELON FAKIE / STARR

TRICK CITY

SICK
SEQUENTIAL
SECTION

HOT SHOES with BUCKY LASEK and MARK ROACH and BUSTER HALTERMAN

ED TEMPLETON
NOSE BONK / STARR

"THE FACE THAT MOVES FIRE HYDRANTS"
ARTWORK BY ROBERT WILLIAMS

SCOOP:
FUTURE
SKATEBOARDS

TODD SHINTO
HOVERBOARD / VAN DUSEN

street
TUFF
BASTARDS

ZOUNDS!

BLITZPEER

HOUSE
OF
WHEELS

BIG DRILL
CAR

HOT
SHOES
ALAN PETERSEN
FRANKIE HILL
ERIC SANDERSON
GEORGE
WATANABE

PEP
BOARDSLIDE / BLOCK

PUSHEAD

INTERVIEW

The inspirational,
imitated, illustrious
illustrator gives his
final interview.

JONAH GUZZI
ONE-FOOTED OLLIE / MOFO

PHOTO
SPECIAL

HOT
SHOES
JOSH
SWINDELL
J.J.
ROGERS

STEVE CABALLERO
FRONTSIDE ROCK AND ROLL SLIDE / MOFO

SKATE
SURF
SPECIAL

EDDIE REATEGUI FRONTSIDE OLLIE / NEEDHAM
INSET: CHRISTIAN FLETCHER OCEANIC OLLIE / SWEGI

MODERN
MOTION

BACKSIDE DISASTER
to SCHOOL ISSUE.

SKATEBOARDS:
HOW THEY
ARE MADE

BRANDON CHAPMAN
BACKSIDE DISASTER / STARR

FREE

HOW
TO
OLLIE

zine
thing
RETURNS

PLUS
DOWNHILL

ALL THIS AND...
SNOWBOARDING TOO!

RAY BARBEE
FRONTSIDE FLIP / SLEEPER

NAKED

PHOTO
SPECIAL

GLOBAL
STOMP
•BRAZIL
Rio de Janeiro
•GERMANY
Munster
•FRANCE
Le Grand Bornand
•USA
Minneapolis
Portland

ERIC DRESSEN
OLLIE NOSE BONK / SLEEPER

SF
OMAR HASSAN vs DANNY WAY
SHOWDOWN

DANNY WAY
MUTE TO FAKIE / ORTIZ

1991

ONE GNARLY DECADE: *Thrasher* is 10 years old. Hawk (our first Skater of the Year, 1990) and Hosoi relive the past. Gonz combs his hair. Back to The City. Jody Foster's Army. Ed Templeton nose bonks an oil drum in Huntington Beach and things haven't been the same since. Guess what: video grabs are the sequence of the moment. Noses are getting bigger. Robert Williams paints us a cover. Nirvana, Jesus Jones, and Skankin' Pickle. Tim Payne shows how to bend plywood. Skateboards of the future, while snowboards are presently huge. Palo Alto is graff-free. Stage diving is in. Skaters in uniform report from Saudi Arabia during Desert Storm. Pushead gives his final interview. Fashionistas victomas: the beginning. Sacto. Joey McSqueeb reports on the makings of urethane and aluminum. Surfing's a sport? Studio 43. Sisters of Mercy. DIY lives: how to make ramps and 'zines. Swindell is a free man. GG. Napalm Death. Public Enemy. Fugazi. As in the beginning, Back to The City again.

Joe Lopes may be dead, but ask anyone who knew him: hyped-out, genuine righteous dude. Rip in peace. Forever ollie in SF at 43

Brown Marble was all the spot. New Deal dude and true SF loc **Rick Ibaseta** sets his back Smith on fire

OGDEN

Maple

FREAKS

OGDEN

Rube, Curtis, and Blake take the turn in the Berkeley Hills

Maple ply was one of the best reasons to ride the Münster ramps. **D Way** never failed to shock the fuck out of the master race; method to fakie

TG made the switch to Real, and the rest is history

KANIGHTS

KANIGHTS

Ever-slick **Julien Stranger** can haul balls on a sled. Mother Earth screams as he sideswipes a wallie off a trunk. Roots, baby; roots

Chicken wing Japan by **Omar Hassan** on his way to victory at the Disco in Frisco

OG EMB nerd **Mike Carroll** shiftys while **Guy** and **Rick** get schooled

Embarco lurks in the park on any given Sunday

LEGEND:
WADE SPEYER

By MIKE CARROLL

MY FIRST MEMORY of Wade was at San Francisco's Embarcadero. He was wearing—I think—a flannel and some tight-ass jeans. It's not that his gear was crazy, it's just that you could tell he didn't care about rocking the newest, coolest Jimmy Z's or Vision gear like most of us young skaters usually did. He was riding a super beat-up board with, if my memory serves me right, a Nosebone Duct-taped to his board and maybe a Tailbone, but I'm not sure about the Tailbone. This was after people stopped using Nosebones, for sure, so I didn't understand why this guy was still rocking one. But the fact that he was fucking ripping all over the place with that Nosebone was the one thing that we all tripped off; only pros ripped that hard, but pros wouldn't be running a Nosebone. And the ollie off the wave over the block! I think it ended up being a sequence in *Thrasher*. None of us knew who this dude was or where he came from. But we definitely talked about him as if he was some legend for a while.

Fast-forward a couple years. It was Wade Speyer! One thing I remember that was pretty funny back in the day is when he stayed at our house. I had Guy, Rudy, and Tim Gavin staying there too. Guy had a two-liter of Coke in the fridge. So one day we came home from skating and Guy goes to get some of his Coke to drink. As he was grabbing the two-liter, Wade had to stop him and said, "I hope you don't mind; I used your Coke bottle to spit my chew in." It's possible that Guy drank Wade's spit.

Anyway, my thoughts on Wade: he's on my list of ultimate skateboarders. He can skate anything at anytime. I don't mean to be all on his jock and compare because there is no comparing in skating, but his skating, to me, is the closest thing you'll get to the Ben Schroeder style—meaning speed, power, and creativity. Fuck a BMW or a Mercedes. How many skaters can say they own a tractor or a Bobcat? Not too many. Wade rips and is a cool-ass dude.

The first knocks on Hubba's door were from **Wade Speyer**. All hail, hell awaits

"HOW MANY SKATERS CAN SAY THEY OWN A TRACTOR OR A BOBCAT?"

Check the eyes as **Hosoi** drifts an alley-oop ollie at Sacto. Control was never an issue

MAIL DROP

Send all info, compliments and criticisms to Mail Drop, THRASHER MAGAZINE, P.O. Box 884570, San Francisco, CA 94188-4570.

SUCKS??

BMX sucks! I'd laugh at someone saying that like I'd laugh at someone wearing a Pac-Man T-shirt. It seems to be the latest trend with skaters to hate BMXers with a passion. I guess it feels macho to hate BMX but the funny thing is that most rad skaters understand that it's not the idea of riding a bike or a skateboard that matters, it's getting rad that matters. Most of the time it's the little pinheads that are trying to be cool skaters that get real into hating BMX. Some smart opportunist out there would make a fortune selling buttons and shirts stating that BMX sucks to all the geeks with shoe-size IQs. Whoever makes this stuff should write it in very large letters so the real skaters can have an easy time spotting all the pinners.

Tom Guerrero, Drobble
SF, CA

DREAM ANALYSIS

Is it abnormal to sleep with your skate every night?

Motorhead
Hingham, MA

Only if you do it out of wedlock. T-ed

...ext time you throw a contest that you ...how some respect for the "older skaters of the sport" by reserving ...em a seat, frontrow, with the name ...judge" on the back. Don't you think ...hey are the only people qualified to judge who is ripping the most that day? Think about it.

The Underground Skate
Movement Cult (U.S.M.C)
(We have a few good men.)

MORE TO THE POINT

In your Sept. ish Mr. Hawk said he didn't think there should be streetstyle contests at all. He also thinks people streetskate because there is a demand for it. I think he should go to hell.

Street Skater
Richmond, VA

SELLING POINTS?

I want this subscription cancelled immediately. I want my ten dollars refunded. *Thrasher* is trash, bizarre, violent, satanic, and sexy.

Jane Fredricks
Mother of a twelve-year-old boy
Cincinnati, OH

Thank you, we're flattered, but it can't compare to the 6 o'clock news. T-ed

...area (a lot of skaters!) keep coming to CROP (Convicts Reaching Out to People) presentations. We just got a $10,000 grant to use on transpo busses and outside coordinating. We're all totally grateful. Getting some local press, too.
Again, your letters were good and they helped. Let me know if I can do anything more.

Mark Rogowski

Give the boot to all kooks, Razor scoots and bean-induced toots at: Mail Drop c/o Thrasher, PO Box 884570 San Francisco, CA 94188-4570

LONG SHOT

...at the hell's the difference between ...ntside and a backside trick? Please ...e us some time and ink and give out ...e community with your valuable ...like wisdom.

Nike Whalen
Las Vegas, NV

...tside means left and backside ...s right. T-ed

BIG BITE

I have always wondered, and people have asked me, why is there the number 23 on the Sal Barbier shoe?

Kyle Brown
Redding, CA

It's his phone number. T-ed

MRS. KAUPAS SPEAKS

Thank you for your excellent coverage of Natas' skating.
I am really distressed that I failed as a mother to teach Natas about his ethnic background and religions in general. Had I explained properly that his grandmother's name is Natalia, a Lithuanian version of Natalie, he never would have said Natasha, which is a diminutive version of Natalie in Russian. You see, the Russian Communists overran the Baltic countries Estonia, Latvia and Lithuania in 1940 as a result of the Stalin-Hitler pact and started murdering and deporting people for merely disagreeing with the Communist doctrine and resisting Russification. Needless to say, we the refugees from the Russian occupation do not want any association whatsoever with their language, culture or ideology.
Lithuanian nouns ending in -a are feminine and the nouns ending in -as are masculine; therefore, Natas could have been named Natalias, but we have abbreviated it to Natas. This has nothing to do with devil worship or religion as such.
We sincerely respect all religious traditions and are fully aware of religion's role in history, teaching ...ble. However, we are ...and believe that we ...harmony without the ...d and devil; although ...oncepts to represent ...d and lowest evil. The ...erman philosopher ...(1724-1804) is closest ...other like gangs, ...se it is obvious that there are still too many mind-controlled, dim-witted, unable-to-comprehend-sarcasm skaters out in the world.
One last thing, just to piss you guys off even more, obviously I've got sponsors and actually get money from skating, and you guys don't. If you guys want, I'll gladly give you the place I currently occupy on my team. Oh yeah, here's my address. If any one of you nameless fools needs to say something, you can do so right to my face. I love being hated.

Tom Knox
728 S Locust, Apt C
Visalia, CA 93277

Get movin'. T-ed

...do you mean from DC, Scott Johnston? Reese Forbes? Yes, they seem to have good personal hygiene, dress well, and, most importantly, are fresh, exciting skateboarders. And, from Philly, Ricky Oyola? Fred Gall? I don't know about funky fresh, but I do know they are dope, exciting skaters you can't fade. But, whatever, it ain't all about who

SPEED FREAKS

This town sucks. Besides the obvious that they play Seal's greatest hits over the loudspeaker during every break at school (it has something to do with reducing violent tendencies). I guess that explains why all the walls are two shades lighter than piss after a couple of Old Milwaukees. To make things worse, there's no place to skate. I don't think anybody even skates in this town anyway. However, there is no ...

HELLO, SUSAN

T-ed, please print this. My girlfriend loves *Thrasher* and I know she'll see it here. I think she's still my girlfriend. She won't return my calls. Thank you.
Dear Susan,
There is something between us lately. We don't communicate like we used to. Don't you remember how I finished your sentences because our thoughts overlapped? I loved you. I love you still. I

OGDEN

From the Visalia wastelands, **Karma Tsocheff** came to SF and got hooked up big time in little time. Bonk da hydrant

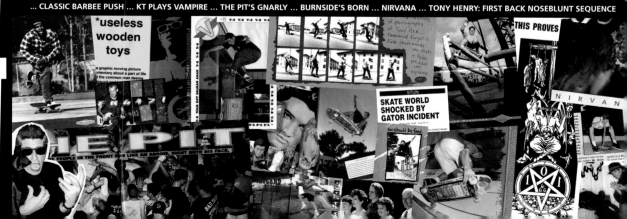

... CLASSIC BARBEE PUSH ... KT PLAYS VAMPIRE ... THE PIT'S GNARLY ... BURNSIDE'S BORN ... NIRVANA ... TONY HENRY: FIRST BACK NOSEBLUNT SEQUENCE

1992

"We don't worship Satan."

—*Slayer*

WADE SPEYER
FRONTSIDE AIR / KANIGHTS

ERIC BRITTON
NOSEGRIND / BLOCK

CHET THOMAS
SHIFTY OLLIE / XENO

RONNIE BERTINO
NOSEBLUNT TRANSFER / DAWES

TOM KNOX OLLIE / SLEEPER
SEQUENCE: JOHN MONTESSI BLUNTSLIDE / THATCHER

PAT DUFFY
FRONTSIDE 180 NOSEGRIND / KANIGHTS

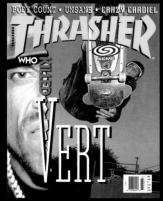

ICE-T PORTRAIT / WIEDERHORN
REMY STRATTON TAILGRAB TO FAKIE / ORTIZ

SEAN SHEFFEY
HEELFLIP SHOVE-IT / ORTIZ

JOVONTAE TURNER
BACKSIDE HEELFLIP / KANIGHTS

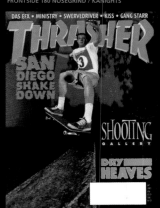

DANIEL POWELL ESQ
NOSEBLUNT SLIDE / ORTIZ

ALPHONSO RAWLS
BACK SMITH / ORTIZ

MIKE CARROLL
CROOKED GRIND / KANIGHTS

1992

HI TOPS GET CHOPPED and pegged pants turn into unhemmed threads. Danny Sargent will work for food. Wheels go sub-50mm. Vancouver, junkstyle, Pearl Jam. *Thrasher*'s staff list off the greatest shows of all time. Danny Way is SOTY 1991. Mike Carroll shelves stroke-it graphics. Hawk chats up Nitzer Ebb. Helmet crushes. Long Beach hosts Sheffey, Thomas, and Campbell. Nose to the grindstone. Dinosaur rock. Ronnie Bertino. Vert is officially dead. Nevermind 50… wheels are near 30mm by the time school's out. Pat Duffy. Salman. Neal Hendrix. Body Count. L7. Cardiel. Pantera. A red polka-dotted filing cabinet makes its way around The City. SF is the capitol of the skateboard world; we got six covers this year! MC Ren on family values. Ten good reasons to start skating: girls. Mike Carroll crooks the Hideout.

Mike Vallely stales in comparison. Barcelona, before it was cool

Big Sally nollie shifties in Santa Barbara. This is some epic shit

Opposite page: **Jovontae Turner** styles for miles at Fort Mason. Good rotation; heelflip landed proper

MIKE KEPPER HOLDS IT DOWN … MINISTRY SUCKS … JEN O'BRIEN GRINDS FRONTSIDE AT THE PLEASANT HILL POOL … THE DWARVES MAKE A LIVING OUT OF 13-MINUTE SHOWS … MON SANDHU GETS THE

FIRST DOCUMENTED SEQUENCE OF A NOLLIE HEELFLIP AT EMB ... GONZ GOES UNDERGROUND ... CARDS 180s A STREET IN THE RAIN ... JOVONTAE TURNER HAD THE HUSTLE DOWN PAT ...

Don't try cornering our photographers on why they liked a particular night of music best; they tend to let the images do the talking. Meanwhile, the writers pull their hair out trying to cram the right words into their allotted space, knowing full well the editors will chop it all to hell anyway. All across the country last year, big concerts and radical musical events went down. Here are the top shows of 1991 according to members of the Thrasher editorial and photographic staff.

GREATEST
SHOWS
ON

Ever-present cast, ever-present dude.
Front board, **Salman**

Gonz goes Picasso

The Oakland Hills fire turned on 23 pools. **Matt Neely** takes one into the shallow at the most popular, Black Bottom.
Rest in peace, Peanut

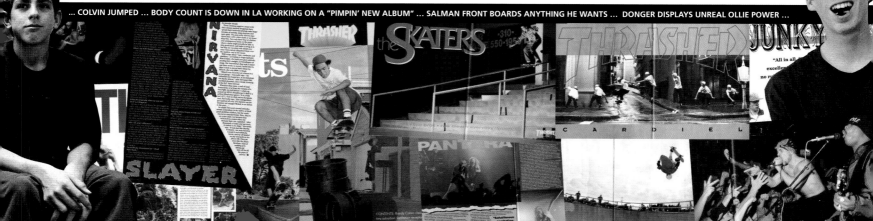

... COLVIN JUMPED ... BODY COUNT IS DOWN IN LA WORKING ON A "PIMPIN' NEW ALBUM" ... SALMAN FRONT BOARDS ANYTHING HE WANTS ... DONGER DISPLAYS UNREAL OLLIE POWER ...

LEGEND:
PAT DUFFY

By DANNY WAY

IN 1991 I SAW Pat Duffy skate for the first time at San Pasqual High School. I skated for H-Street, and towards the end of that (right before we started Plan B) I kept hearing these crazy stories about him: stories about big handrails, huge gaps, and just the craziest stuff that anyone had ever done. He was amateur, so we had an opportunity when we started Plan B to take him from H-Street and put him on the team. In order for Pat to join, though, he had to be voted in by everyone on Plan B; therefore, Pat had to come down and skate with the entire team. Not everyone had heard about him yet, and no one had seen him skate in person. Those who had heard about him only knew of him through these crazy stories that had been passed along—and no one knew if these stories were true or not.

We all went to San Pasqual High School one day to check Pat out. It was crazy because we put him in a pressure situation. We had all the guys from Plan B, which was a well-recognized team, watching him perform to see if he was capable of being on with us. There was doubt before going to watch him, but the stuff Pat did that day was mind blowing. We looked at each other and were speechless about where skateboarding was heading after we saw him skate. Pat Duffy, for years to come, revolutionized and pushed skating's boundaries further than anybody in the street world, to the point where his name remains legendary.

The kid from nowhere about to go everywhere, **Pat Duffy** back Smiths at SF State. This four-stair was one of the first sessioned handrails

"HIS NAME REMAINS LEGENDARY"

Talk about gnar: **Cards** smoked some herb and made history. Snaps, baby

CARDS vs
THE GONZ

I GOT A CALL from John Lucero, asking me for some photos for my first Black Label ad. I told him I was on it and I started thinking about what I could do. I called Tobin Yelland and asked him if anyone had backside 180'd the Gonz at EMB. He said no, so I asked him if he'd shoot photos of me trying it. "Sure," he

"I WAS POSSESSED ON THIS TRICK"

said, and that next morning I woke up, gave my friend Hanzy Driscoll a call, and we bolted down to the Embarcadero.

I was possessed on this trick. I skated around for a minute and then climbed up on the ledge; it took me like three or four tries until I landed it. Henry Sanchez ran up to me and gave me five. I was feeling good! We went up to Haight Street, hooked up with some friends, and I told them what I'd just done. Wheatberry bought me a beer and we kicked back and watched girls on one of the best days I've had in The City. —*John Cardiel*

The Candy Man, **John Cardiel**, snatches a frontside and bones it out at Blockhead Ramp. The Earth shook

... TOMMY G WINS CITY HALL AND GIVES HIS FAKE CHECK TO CARROLL ... SWERVEDRIVER, DAS EFX, METALLICA ... DAN ROGERS GETS OUT THE PARACHUTES ... FRED GALL PHONES HOME ... WATT SOUNDS OFF ...

KANIGHTS

FISCHER

Jason Jessee, 1954

KANIGHTS

Curtis Hsiang had the face and the balls to make just about anything…just about. Thruster at the Hook

THE 5,000-FOOT GIRL ATTACKS ... THE INDOOR POOL IN OAKLAND HAS MANY BLACK MASS CANDLES, DEAD CATS, AND HELLA SPOOKY SHIT ... MEATBALLS DON'T BOUNCE, THEY SPLAT

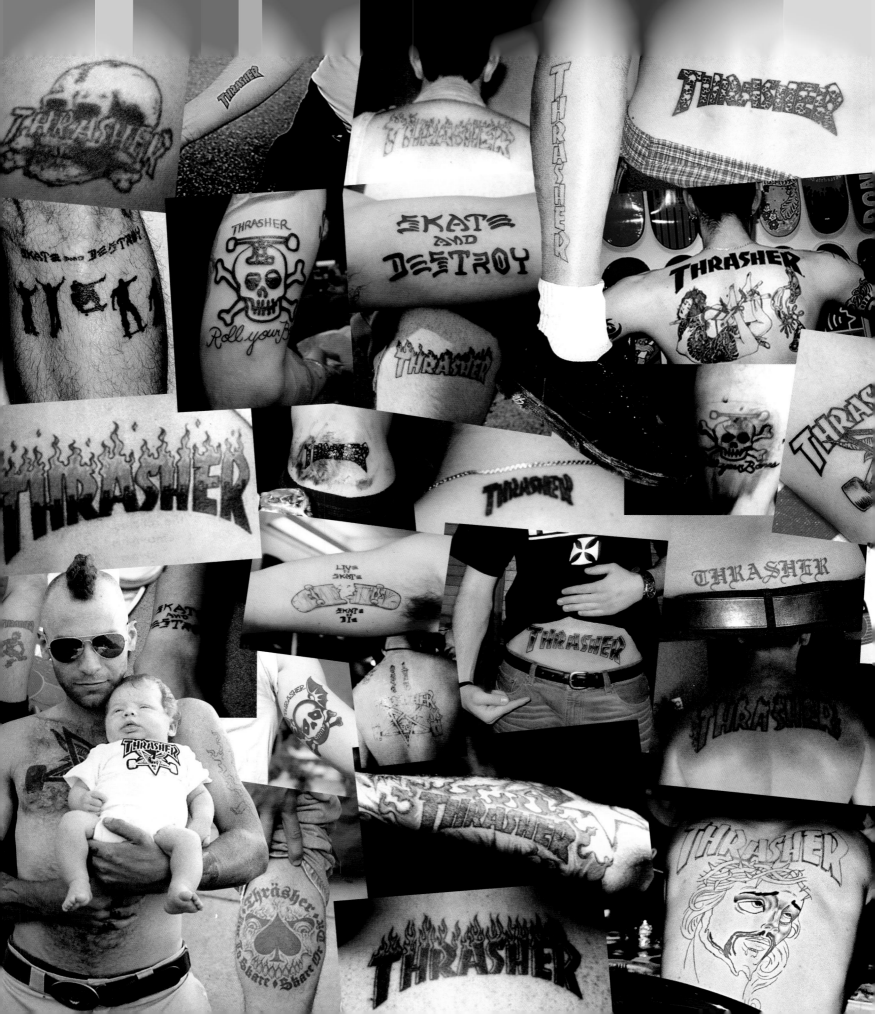

HOW MANY other mags get inked? *Thrasher* is the only real choice. Down For Life, and we don't mean prison

1993

"Everything I own is in this bag."
—*GG Allin*

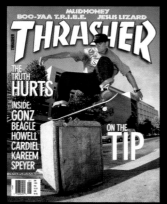

TIM BRAUCH
NOSEGRIND / KANIGHTS

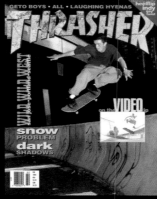

JEFF PANG BACKSIDE SHIFTY / ORTIZ
INSET: COCO SANTIAGO HEELFLIP

RICK IBASETA
50-50 / KANIGHTS

JOHN CARDIEL
HOOP OF FIRE / KANIGHTS

JULIEN STRANGER
BACKSIDE LIPSLIDE / KANIGHTS

MARK GONZALES
FRONTSIDE OLLIE / KANIGHTS

HENRY SANCHEZ
HEELFLIP FRONTSIDE NOSESLIDE / KANIGHTS

JOE SIERRO OLLIE / DOLINSKY
JASON ADAMS NOSEGRIND / KANIGHTS
JUSTIN ORTIZ FAKIE 360 FLIP / ORTIZ

KARMA TSOCHEFF
180 NOSEGRIND TO FORWARD / SEAN DOLINSKY

"TOMBSTONE"
LOGO BY JIMBO

RICK HOWARD
SWITCH 360 FLIP / KANIGHTS

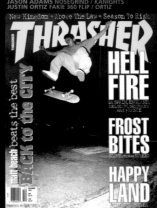

ERIC KOSTON
FRONTSIDE FLIP / MORRIS

1993

VIDEO GRABS SATURATE ads and editorial content, a good 10 years before digital cameras send film on its way to a slow death. Cardiel is SOTY and blasts the sea wall at Ocean Beach in celebration. Jeans are industrial, thick, and huge, hat bills are flat. Flannels are buttoned at the neck. Danny Way: heelflip indy gay twist. Wade Speyer: 30-foot crooks. Ronnie Bertino: frontside noseslide nollie flip to fakie. We teach you how to get laid, sponsored, and paid. Gator and Swindell head to the Big House. Gonz gets back to his roots. Jazz Matazz. Bosstones. Mudhoney. Jesus Lizard. Geto Boys. Tool. Primus. Brand Nubian. Ice T. The mag issues number 150. Two months later, after 50 years, skateboarding dies. We mourn by sending razor blades in candy bars to ASR.

Gonz came back on radar after his radical sabbatical, lamenting his "Alzheimer's." He was 24. Half-flip back tail

SF has always had the terrain; we just called 'em out. Many showed up, some got. Frequent flier **John Cardiel** came, saw, and snapped while the neighbors looked on. A Salman embroidered Camel jersey and 40mm Spits. If you were around then, you know

KANIGHTS

Jason Adams crooky monsters a tall juice box

YELLAND

"This cat's name is **Trouble**"

Brown Marble was the spot for all the shots. **Mike Daher** kickflips the planter

SCOTT JOHNSTON: FRONT CROOKS HUBBA ... ROYCE BLASTS BLACK BOTTOM ... GONZ USES SPRAY-ON GRIP ... POWELL PERALTA GETS INTO BOY BANDS ... STRANGER OWNS SAFEWAY ... NY DOGS INVADE SF ...

LEGEND: SALMAN AGAH

By BRIAN ANDERSON

WHEN I FIRST SAW Salman's skating it was in the Powell video *Ban This*. He and Jovontae Turner were skating around different spots with each other. I really liked this, as the rest of the video was more staged-looking. I could tell Salman was a genuine, raw, street skater. I was always impressed by how relaxed he looked for how big he was. *Nobody* could skate switch like him at the time. People couldn't understand it. He was nollieing higher than anyone in the world. A pioneer of switch, always wanting to just show up, skate as hard as he could and have fun—Salman Agah is a true street skateboarder. Try to get your hands on the first Real video.

"NOBODY COULD SKATE SWITCH LIKE HIM"

When we sent this ad to our printer, they stopped the presses 'cause they thought it was flopped— it ain't. Beastly switch snaps

BRIAN
BRANNON

IN THE EARLY '90s, a new era dawned in skateboarding as a burgeoning tide of street skaters pushed aside the old guard of pool hounds and vert dogs. Where once the sultans of slash denigrated the flippity-dippity fancy footwork of the tight-shorts-wearing freestyle crew, it was the flatlanders who had the last laugh as street skating took hold.

Previously ignored and deplored, the freestyle mafia sowed the seeds of its revenge, served cold as curb slappies and ollies took hold across the land. No longer was skateboarding limited to rich kids with ramps and outlaws barging ditches, pipes, and pools. Round walls were disregarded in favor of a level playing field accessible to any skater in Anytown, USA: the street.

The apparent mastermind behind this big takeover was a shadowy character by the name of Steve Rocco. Back in the 1980s, when street skating was still something to do on the way to the liquor store, he was seen decked out in new wave attire in Sims ads doing inverts off slanted curbs and two-inch-high backside airs on slight sidewalk inclines.

Turning the tables on every carve-grinding coping killer who ever snickered when a freestyler spacewalked by, Rocco ushered in a new regime where wheel sizes shriveled, board widths withered, and the music of choice went from hardcore punk to gangster rap. The mocked became the mockers. It was in with baggy pants and down with punk rockers.

Thrasher rolled with the changes as it struggled to remain true to the heart and soul of skateboarding. A four-eyed loudmouth who called bullshit as he saw

fit was brought up from the shipping department to take over the editorial reins and keep the ship of skate on course as it headed into harm's way.

Jake Phelps not only knew every trick and every skater who had ever appeared in any skate mag on the planet, he could tell you what issue and which article it was in as well. What's more, he had a handle on those who had yet to grace the pages, as well as a keen eye to discern what was worthy in both the new style and the old.

After laying the groundwork for the spirit and attitude of the best damn skateboard mag of all time, founding fathers Mofo and KT graciously stepped aside and let the new breed take hold. Bryce Kanights became the keeper of the darkroom flame and your humble narrator flipped the switch on the sound system as music editor. Despite all the changes that were tumbling down around us, it was a good time to be a skateboarder. In fact, I am happy to say that I have yet to see a period when it was a bad time to be a skateboarder. When skateboarding is booming, new parks sprout up left and right, and skaters get the respect and paychecks they deserve. When times are tough, we weed out the fakers and takers and haters, leaving only the real skaters, whether they ride street, pools, or vert.

In the end it doesn't matter what you ride, it's all skateboarding. And through it all, *Thrasher* will remain the no-bullshit zone, whose hallowed pages tell tales of true skateboarding in all its rough and ragged glory.

Long live *Thrasher* mag. Cheers to 25 more years. —*Brian Brannon*

"IN THE END IT DOESN'T MATTER WHAT YOU RIDE, IT'S ALL SKATEBOARDING. AND THROUGH IT ALL, THRASHER WILL REMAIN THE NO-BULLSHIT ZONE"

Opposite page: True Skate & Destroy champ **Shorty Gonzales** back tail front bluntslides a Fisherman's Wharf double-sider in front of a young Martha Stewart

... KEENAN GETS A VENTURE AD RIDING THUNDERS ... GONZ KICKFLIPS THE GONZ IN FRONT OF JAMIE THOMAS ... WAY NOSESLIDES BROOKLYN BRIDGE RAIL WITH A HIGH FEVER ... GINO IANNUCCI BACKSIDE HEELFLIPS THE GONZ

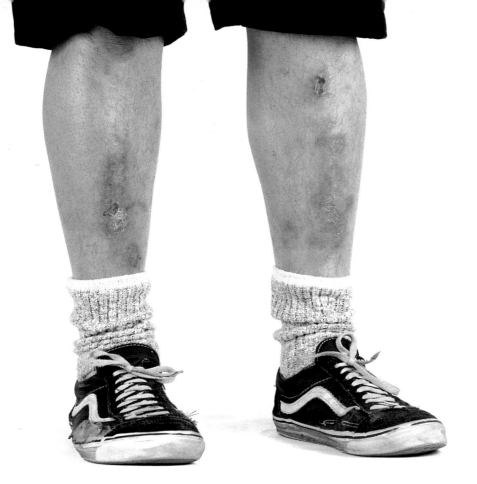

1994

"I've been put in skateboarding."

—*Salman Agah*

OFX ✦ PITT ✦ KRS-1 ✦ MORBID ANGEL ✦ STATIC

THRASHER

SK AVALON

RTH vs SOUTH
D's AWARDS

special issue

THIRTEEN
years down

ARL SHIPMAN FRONT BLUNT / KANIGHTS
SET: AVALON JOHNSON

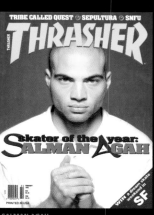

TRIBE CALLED QUEST ✪ SEPULTURA ✪ SNFU

THRASHER

skater of the year:
SALMAN AGAH

WIN a mega skate
weekend in
SF

SALMAN AGAH
SOTY PORTRAIT / MADEO

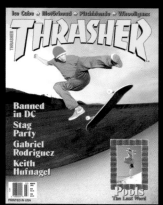

Ice Cube ✦ Motörhead ✦ Pitchblende ✦ Whooligans

THRASHER

Banned
in DC

Stag
Party

Gabriel
Rodriguez

Keith
Hufnagel

Pools
The Last Word

JASON ADAMS KICKFLIP FAKIE 15 FEET UP / KANIGHTS
INSET: REMY STRATTON EGGPLANT / KANIGHTS

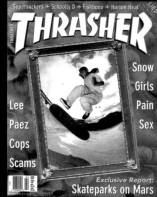

Supersuckers ✦ Schoolly D ✦ Fishbone ✦ Horton Heat LIES

THRASHER

Snow

Girls

Lee   Pain
Paez
Cops   Sex

Scams

Exclusive Report:
Skateparks on Mars

JAIME REYES
360 FLIP / STARR

De La Soul • George Clinton • Snowboard Tricks

THRASHER

HEY,
DO I
LOOK LIKE
A STREET
SKATER?

HEY, DO I LOOK LIKE A STREET SKATER?"
TWORK BY MARK GONZALES

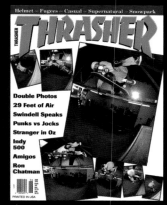

Helmet ∼ Fugees ∼ Casual ∼ Supernatural ∼ Snowpark

THRASHER

Double Photos
29 Feet of Air
Swindell Speaks
Punks vs Jocks
Stranger in Oz
Indy
500
Amigos
Ron
Chatman

MIKE FRAZIER
KICKFLIP MUTE / KANIGHTS

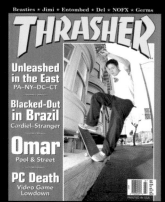

Beasties ★ Jimi ★ Entombed ★ Del ★ NOFX ★ Germs

THRASHER

Unleashed
in the East
PA–NY–DC–CT

Blacked-Out
in Brazil
Cardiel-Stranger

Omar
Pool & Street

PC Death
Video Game
Lowdown

JAYA BONDEROV
NOSEGRIND / MARTINEAU

NAS ✦ MEAT PUPPETS ✦ COOLIO ✦ MARXMAN ✦ SLAMS

THRASHER

PAVED
NEW
WORLD

MATT PAILES
WILD RIDE / BUTLER

HOUSE OF PAIN ✦ RAW FUSION ✦ MIKE WATT ✦ AFRO-PLANE

THRASHER

War
with
Satan

BANNED

Barbee & Mandoli
on Christianity

DY ROY LIEN / SEDWAY
SET: GRANT MINOR DOWNSHIFTY
F ROCK FACE / BING

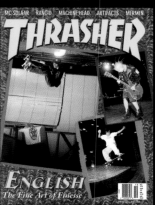

MC SOLAAR ∼ RANCID ∼ MACHINE HEAD ∼ ARTIFACTS ∼ MERMEN

THRASHER

ENGLISH
The Fine Art of Finesse

BOB BURNQUIST
FRONTSIDE AIR / LEFT 1

LINT
FISCHER

DAVE DUREN
FAKIE 5-0 / KANIGHTS

G LOVE ✦ KILLDOZER ✦ MOTOCASTER ✦ BRAND NUBIAN

THRASHER
Air Raid

Road Kill: Pennsylvania & Colorado

ALAN PETERSEN
OLLIE / KANIGHTS

BOOTSY ✦ BOSSTONES ✦ SUICIDAL ✦ TAD ✦ GAS HUFFER

THRASHER

WADE
BURNS
EUROPE

WADE SPEYER
METHOD / KANIGHTS

N'S front blunt down
summarizes the world.
print for 13 years.
with huge switch blasts
ted wrist. The mag hires
on-the-eyes member of
ni team, to advise the
wboarding is banned.
ne second girl on the cover,
d Hawaiian 360 flip. Gibo's
d. Skateboarding goes
ultiple trips to the Southern
Bob on the cover. The
e a mini-ramp in the music
Coast is where it's at:
NYC, DC, CT. Bootsy. Jimi.
eat of the summer. NOFX.
planetary expeditions.
ple set forever.

ou experienced?

fakie back tails a decent-sized
s had the real pop

Royce Nelson backside, backyard, bananas

JUSTIN BOKMA PUTS TORONTO ON THE MAP ... SIMON IS CLASS CLOWN ... PEPE MARTINEZ RULES PULASKI IN DC ... FABIO IN THE MAG? ... SARGE, BEHIND THE 8-BALL AND LOVING IT ... OMAR OLLIES TO FAKIE AT BELMAR'S ...

'**Reem** claims Westside. True legend

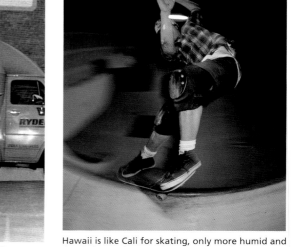

"Heru sick" is how **Mike Cao** would describe this frontside noseslide

Hawaii is like Cali for skating, only more humid and the dudes are just a tad on the gnar side. Islander **Stacey Gibo**—bloodied, battered Smith in SF

In the winter, SF is a ghost town. **Julien Stranger** FSO over the bench in Chinatown on the last day of the year

JOHN CARDIEL

By JULIEN STRANGER

I NEED TO MAKE SURE I don't waste any words. No, not that. I need to not use any flowery language, no clichés, that the words are cut down and fundamental. Okay.

At one point I thought I was better than John. It was the heart behind the skating that I must not have thought mattered. In the blind competitiveness of youth, all I saw were tricks or something. What a retard. Through time I've seen again and again displays of cojones and determination that were obviously beyond me or anyone I know. Okay, that's it. No more words. Words are abstractions like time and money.

No, there's more.

There is a love for skating that even few life-long skaters have. Maybe it's not love, because I know we all love skating, but maybe it's the intensity of that feeling that not all of us have, but that John and a few others do have. Maybe I just don't have it. It's easy to love to skate and have a good time when it's good, but I've seen JC having the worst sessions ever—hard, bad, kooky slams over and over—and not stop. When any normal skater would pick up their board and call it a day, JC is unable to quit. For real, unable. There is only the now, and in that is one of the not-so-secret reasons why John rips so hard and why he has made his mark on skateboarding, like a curb blasted into oblivion by the slappy god of concrete under his wheels. Wait, that was extreme flowery language. Oh well, we'll just leave it and maybe get a laugh out of it later.

The force of will to overcome defeat makes John "John Cardiel."

Sacto pools are hot and sticky; **John Cardiel** is as well. Smoke 'em frontside corner shot

"THE FORCE OF WILL TO OVERCOME DEFEAT"

The Widowmaker bites the blade, but not before **Tas Pappas** nollie heelflips to fakie

Smoothy **Phil Shao** snaps off Granview bump in SF

Ground Zero after 9-11 is James Lick schoolyard (Clipper ledge is in back). **Coco Santiago** 180 nosegrinds the other side

BRYCE KANIGHTS

MY INVOLVEMENT with *Thrasher* first began with extensive stints locked in a darkroom while cranking punk rock on a boom box, developing film, and churning out prints. This was when *Thrasher* was the primary catalyst that ignited a dead

"I'M STOKED TO HAVE CONTRIBUTED TO THE CAUSE"

skateboard industry in the early '80s. I often swept floors and emptied trash bins, too, and from those first initiatory years of toiling with Photostats, X-Acto knives, wax, rubylithes and overlays, it all seems a bit symbolic to me now. Those were fundamental moments in shaping a movement, a revolution if you will, that would carry onward to the future. I'm stoked to have contributed to the cause and played a major function over the years.

Sincere thanks to KT, Mofo, Fausto, Eric, Ed, Jake, Luke, Burnett, and the rest of *Thrasher*'s staff past and present for keeping skateboarding's principles just where they belong—with the skaters. See you out there. —*Bryce Kanights*

Sean Sheffey nosegrinds on tiny wheels and rattling bolts

... RICH JOHNSON & JUICE ARE WILD IN WYOMING ... BURNETT COMES ON RADAR CRAILSLIDING IN COLORADO ... CARROLL KICKFLIPS TOWNSEND, YOU CAN HEAR HIS FOOT HIT THE GRIP ... 20-MAN DROP AT THE WIDOWMAKER

1995

"I love the sport."

—*Tina Paez*

Duane & Jay & Karma & Paez & Frazier & Hendrix

THRASHER

Know
the Past...
Seize the
Future

MIKE CONWAY
NOSESLIDE / MARTINEAU

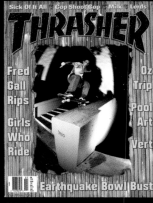

Sick Of It All • Cop Shoot Bop • Milk • Lords

THRASHER

Fred
Gall
Rips

Girls
Who
Ride

Oz
Trip

Pool
Art

Vert

Earthquake Bowl Bust

FRED GALL
SWITCH FRONTSIDE 5-0 / MORF

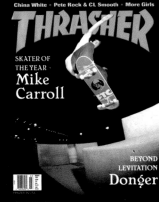

China White • Pete Rock & CL Smooth • More Girls

THRASHER

SKATER OF
THE YEAR
Mike
Carroll

BEYOND
LEVITATION
Donger

MIKE CARROLL
GAP TO FRONTSIDE TAILSLIDE / KANIGHTS

SLAYER • KURT COBAIN–FROM THE GRAVE • HURRICANE

THRASHER

ARTWORK BY SEAN MCKNIGHT, AGE 7

BIG CHIEF • JACKYL • FARSIDE • ROLLING STONE

THRASHER

DOWN
SOUTH

SLUGGO

TEXAS

TOM
BOYLE

SICK SWITCH VERT

MAX SCHAAF
HALF-CAB / CALLAN

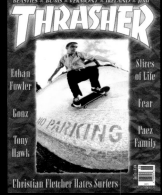

BEASTIES • BUMS • VERMONT • IRELAND • JIMI

THRASHER

Ethan
Fowler

Gonz

Tony
Hawk

Slices
of Life

Fear

Paez
Family

Christian Fletcher Hates Surfers

ETHAN FOWLER
SWITCH WALLRIDE / MORF

NEW BOMB TURKS • WAX • VEGAS • TAMPA • HIRATA

THRASHER

Cult of
the Longboard

CR STECYK III
TOES ON THE NOSE / STECYK

SANTANA • SANTA ROSA • VANCOUVER • BOSTON

THRASHER

MEET THE
BOMB SQUAD

PHIL SHAO
SMITH / KANIGHTS

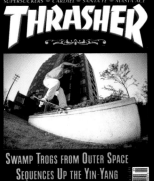

SUPERSUCKERS • CARDIEL • SANTA FE • MASTA ACE

THRASHER

SWAMP TROGS FROM OUTER SPACE
SEQUENCES UP THE YIN-YANG

MOSES ITKONEN
SWITCH TAILSLIDE / SERFAS

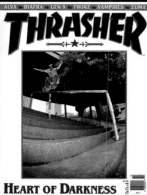

ALVA • BIAFRA • GEN X • TWINZ • VAMPIRES • ZUMA

THRASHER

HEART OF DARKNESS

CHAD MUSKA
5-0 / DALGART

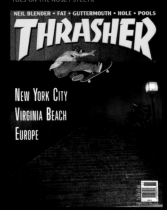

NEIL BLENDER • FAT • GUTTERMOUTH • HOLE • POOLS

THRASHER

NEW YORK CITY

VIRGINIA BEACH

EUROPE

QUIM CARDONA
FRONTSIDE AIR / MORF

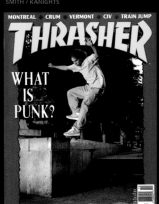

MONTREAL • CRUM • VERMONT • CIV • TRAIN JUMP

THRASHER

WHAT
IS
PUNK?

MIKE BOUCHARD
FRONTSIDE NOSEGRIND / RYAN

1995

ALONG WITH THE WHEELS, skating gets bigger again. And faster and smoother. Skaters who embody these traits grace the covers: Ethan Fowler, Mike Carroll (SOTY), Fred Gall, Bob Burnquist. Phil Shao stands up frontside on top of 10 feet, no water. Rosa's phone number is in the mag. Kurt Cobain sends a message from heaven directly to our readers. A seven-year-old draws us a cover. An all-out assault on heavier ledges, rails, and drops begins. You're either burly, a jock, well-groomed, or an art jazz goatee'd dude. We covered this new festival called the Warped Tour and it was pretty cool. Stereo. Masta Ace. Slayer. Farside. CIV. Punk is frontside double kinks and sharing a beer with a friend. Vampires, once a staple and center of debate, slowly fade from Mail Drop. The Pipe Dream revolution, where cities build decent concrete parks, is in its infancy. Fortunately for us, Santa Rosa is a short drive north.

Why was everyone coming to SF? This photo says it all: **Scott Johnston**, snappy-do into the steepness

Chad Muska had yet to be on Shorty's, but even back then he could throw down from there to here

CHAZ MCGEE, SMOOTH LIL' BROTHER ... FRANK FERRET GARCIA GETS AN INTERVIEW, HIS WIFE COMPLAINS ... CHAD MUSKA TILTS HIS HAT SIDEWAYS, LEAVES MAPLE ... LENNY KIRK, SWITCH BACKSIDE 5-0 HUBBA ...

THE VERY BEST OF ETHAN FOWLER

What's Neat & What's Beat

NEAT	BEAT	NEAT	BEAT	NEAT	BEAT
Hills	Malls	Dip	Smokes	Chiseling	Tagging
Hair	Baldness	Nohawks	Mohawks	Sheaths	Rubbers
Scars	Scabs	Impaling	Piercing	The Finger	Peace
Branding	Tattoos	Unicycles	Mopeds	Slingshots	Guns
Jail	College	Manners	Barging	Pivots	Stalls
Suspenders	Belts	8-Tracks	CDs	Bikes	Trikes
Cords	Denim	Costumes	Uniforms	Books	Videos
Large	XL	Paying	Shoplifting	Music	Noise
Monocles	Shades	Coffee	Tea	Chugging	Barfing

lenny kirk

LEGEND:
MIKE CARROLL

By MARC JOHNSON

SOMEONE, **ANYONE**, could easily be a better choice assigned to write about Mike Carroll. We've been on a few tours. I saw him at Scott's wedding. I see him around the Girl camp from time to time. We shake hands and I rub his back while he gives me advice. I have no crazy stories about Mikey, but I've heard a lot of them. He's a pretty quiet guy, actually, but you can look at him and see that his gears are always turning. Oh, but what he wants to say—and doesn't. Scary. What else needs to be said about Mike? Top-tier, with the gifts you wish Christmas had brought your way.

The skateboarding goes back to the first video I ever saw, *Hokus Pokus*. Mike was in it. Ripping, 1990. Fuuukin' tearing it up. The game was deep. Carroll is from a practically dead era of skateboarding. Can you remember back when skateboarders were individuals? Remember that creative era? Remember self-expression through skating? Mike never lost that aspect of riding. I like that about him. No half-stepping. He still just does what he wants and does everything nice and proper; never signed up for the rat race. When Punker Johnny was in diapers, Carroll was inventing the stuff. Disposable stunt chumps should take a lesson in longevity and originality from the man himself.

I can't lick the dude's balls; nothing more needs to be said. Learn how to read, get some magazines, watch some videos, attend a demo. Wash your black jeans off, think for yourself, and try to stick around for a while—lots of dudes breeze through the machine like fallen leaves. Carroll is the redwood, the oak, the big monument in the civic square of Shred City. Get up, get down. The dude is OG. You just can't fade that kind of history. After a certain point words do no justice; it just is. Thanks, Mikey, for laying it down since day one.

Mike Carroll is bad to the bone; back Smith on the original Hubba Hideout

"TAKE A LESSON IN LONGEVITY AND ORIGINALITY"

Marc Johnson, crooked grind in Oakland, very early in his battle for victory. The best feet in the business

A taste of the Brits, **Geoff Rowley** blindside flips at Radlands

Union Square saw some great skating.
Ethan Fowler, tall 50-50

Below: Killa **Josh Kalis**, nosegrind to fakie.
Ruben Orkin, "Pay this fool!"

Tony Hawk gets embryonic with a torqued mute in Carson, CA

MC was SOTY, Phelps in a suit; wrong clothes, right guy

Mark Gonzales can do it while he's sleeping. Maybe he is

Opposite page: Sacto, Bitch! Snaggle frontside 5-0s on the hip to fakie, and you are from where?

... CARDS BONES AT SALLY ROSA ... SCHROEDER TALKS ABOUT HIS BROKEN NECK ... GLUEHEAD GETS ARTSY ... PUNK IS BUNK ... DRAKE JONES BUTTERFLIES STRAIGHT WÜSSBERGER ... HEDDINGS RULES BURNSIDE

"AND YOU ARE FROM WHERE?"

1996

"Mark was the first to grind a handrail." —*Natas Kaupas*

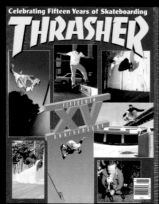

Celebrating Fifteen Years of Skateboarding

THRASHER

FIFTEENTH XV ANNIVERSARY

15TH ANNIVERSARY
*SEE BELOW RIGHT

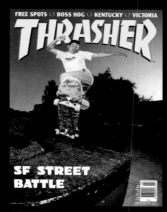

FREE SPOTS ◊ BOSS HOG ◊ KENTUCKY ◊ VICTORIA

THRASHER

SF STREET BATTLE

JUSTIN STRUBING
SALAD GRIND / OGDEN

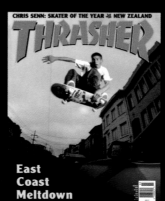

CHRIS SENN: SKATER OF THE YEAR ◊ NEW ZEALAND

THRASHER

East Coast Meltdown

RON WHALEY
JR FRONTSIDE / KANIGHTS

GATOR TALKS ◊ MOST HATED SKATERS ◊ DEAD LAST

THRASHER

Bride of Grindenstein

"BRIDE OF GRINDENSTEIN"
ARTWORK BY MARK DESALVO

STEAL THIS MAGAZINE

THRASHER

POOLS • PIPES • PARKS • PORTLAND • POSERS • PIGS • and even POETRY

COCO SANTIAGO
FRONTSIDE THRUSTER / KANIGHTS

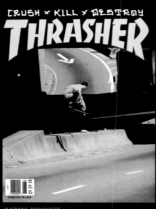

CRUSH × KILL × DESTROY

THRASHER

KARMA TSOCHEFF
BACKSIDE SHIFTY / KANIGHTS

Houston • Machines • Humpers

THRASHER

PHIL SHAO
FRONTSIDE GRIND / OGDEN

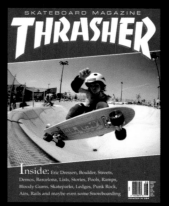

SKATEBOARD MAGAZINE

THRASHER

Inside: Eric Dressen, Boulder, Streets, Demos, Barcelona, Lists, Stories, Pools, Ramps, Bloody Gums, Skateparks, Ledges, Punk Rock, Airs, Rails and maybe even some Snowboarding

ERIC DRESSEN
FRONTSIDE THRUSTER / BRUCE HAZELTON

LAGWAGON • GOLDFINGER • LOUDMOUTHS

THRASHER

JONATHAN BOHANNON
ARTWORK BY GOMEZ BUENO

NEW ORLEANS • DE LA SOUL • SCOTLAND • NUDE BOWL

THRASHER

MARK HUBBARD
BACKSIDE OLLIE / OGDEN

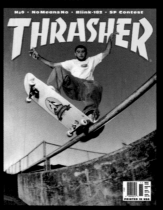

H₂0 • No Means No • Blink-182 • SF Contest

THRASHER

MIKE YORK
FRONTSIDE BLUNTSLIDE TO FAKIE / OGDEN

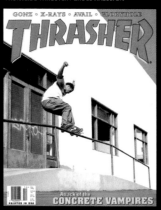

GONE • X-RAYS • AVAIL • GLORYHOLE

THRASHER

Attack of the CONCRETE VAMPIRES

SEAN SHEFFEY
50-50 / OGDEN

1996

FIFTEEN YEARS DOWN. Duane, Tommy, Tony, Holmes, Salman, Cab, and tons more reflect. Two non-skateboarding covers this year—one of the Bride of Grindenstein's 50-50 and one of our neighborhood friend, Jonathan Bohannon—plus a circa-'77 Dressen classic. Glory Hole. Steal our magazine, we don't care. Karma. Mark Gonzales is in the midst of what would become a fine literary tradition: monthly fictional accounts of the non-sense, often illegible, often over-literate. Fresh Jive begins the best page-one ad campaign of all time. The Beatles are the Bones Brigade. Our kids sure can draw; future Art Director Nico Berry has an envelope of the month. SF builds a "skatepark" for the city's riders and Phelper gets to press the flesh with Willie Brown. H2O. White Zombie. No Means No. Sean Sheffey.

One of the most amazing skaters of all time, **Sean Sheffey** came from Back East and took Cali down. Tall IE 50-50

GATOR EXPLAINS KILLING SOMEONE … CRUM OLLIES HIGHER THAN MOST … BOSS HOG, DE LA SOUL, BAD BRAINS … RED RIPS WARM SPRINGS POOL WITH "CHEATER" (CORNER) AIRS … TIM UPSON GETS SENSITIVE …

OGDEN
OGDEN

The Bridge Ramp burned down, but not before **Bob Gnar** got some. Boy did he kill the joint. Everyone sits down for this indy. HRC 1996

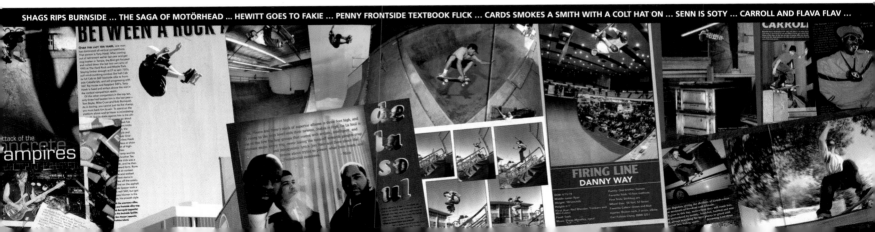

The Maritime Hall in San Francisco had some sick vert sessions. The boys, the beer, and the bands—too sick. **Citizen Stranger**, indy to fakie

Coco tells **Phelps**: "You are about this close…"

Don't laugh, he's crazy. **Sheff**

Ben Sanchez was the East Bay EMB connection. Noseblunt slide at Aquatic Park, SF

Opposite page: Hellrides are like pillage runs. When **Ethan Fowler** signed on in 1996, he didn't know or care; rode the same board the whole time, brought no extra socks. Marseille before it died

LEGEND:
CHRIS SENN

By OMAR HASSAN

RISING FROM THE DEPTHS of Grass Valley, CA, Chris Senn is one of the best that skateboarding has to offer. Chris has unique style, speed, tech, and skates with full aggression and confidence. Through the decades of skating's history, Chris has influenced it with his artistic view by pushing the limits, adapting, and progressing through years of skating's transitional times and eras. Chris has proven to be one of the best all-around skaters, ripping whatever crosses his path, always pushing the limits. Through the '90s Chris dominated—whether it was a video part, contest, demo, or just another day at the park. Chris has always been on top and in the forefront. He seems as stoked on life as he is on skating, always smiling and skating for all the right reasons. Now it's 2005 and Chris continues to push and progress. The respect he has earned through longevity gives him the right to be in the league of legends. If you have a chance to see Chris skate, it's total devastation every time he stands on his board. As Jay Adams would say, he's 100-percent skateboarder. The Chris Senn saga continues.

Chris Senn is all arms and legs over the onion at the Münster Bowl. Foaming at the mouth, pushing uphill and shit

"TOTAL DEVASTATION EVERY TIME HE STANDS ON HIS BOARD"

AM I EVIL?
THE SK8 GOAT STORY

I DREW THE LOGO to put on shirts for the Last Hell Ride party in '94 when the city of Oakland decided to put a new freeway (to replace the one that crumbled in '89) right through Jake's warehouse which at the time housed the infamous Widowmaker vert ramp.

"TWO TIMES MORE EVIL THAN A PENTAGRAM"
—GLUEHEAD

The shirts actually ended up being a different logo with a seven pointed star around the goat head with one flaming and bleeding eyeball in the middle. That logo was a collaboration of my logo and one that was drawn by Gluehead that Jake decided was "more evil." Glue's original (drawn directly on a shirt) can be seen on the cover of the October '94 issue, and my logo (just slightly altered) along with the blow by blow of the party's inside that same issue. The *Thrasher* logo was incorporated into the first version I drew and introduced to the public in October '97. First it was on T-shirts, then eventually on stickers, patches, and sweatshirts. —*Peter Turner*

Sure Shot **Lavar McBride** stands up and pushes the back foot on a City noseslide

... GIRLS INVADE THE PIT ... HOLLYWOOD VERT, HAWK WINS ... COLPITTS DESTROYS EVERYTHING IN SIGHT ... WADE SPEYER COULD REALLY CARE LESS ABOUT WHAT YOU THINK

PHOTOGRAFFITI IS what it is—fools busting and punks snapping flicks. Some are epic, some just suck. Our fave photo credit? "Mom."

1997

"I'm pretty interested in learning."
—*Bobby Puleo*

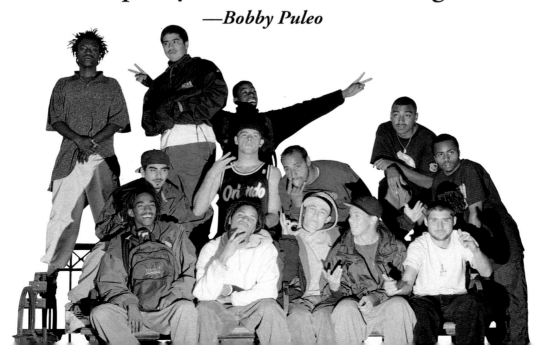

DANNY GONZALEZ
BLASTER / MORF

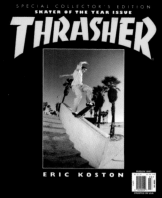

SCOTT JOHNSTON
CROOKED GRIND / OGDEN

ERIC KOSTON
FRONTSIDE NOSEBLUNT SLIDE / OGDEN

MARK GONZALES
POLE JAM / MORF

QUIM CARDONA
FRONTSIDE OLLIE / MORF

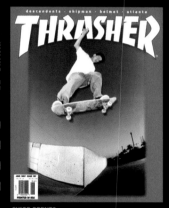

CHICO BRENES
GAP TO BACK TAIL / OGDEN

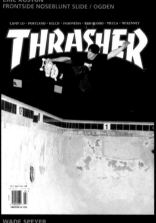

WADE SPEYER
FRONTSIDE AIR / OGDEN

BOBBY PULEO
Snapcase
CHICAGO
Boot Camp Clik
CHEESEHEADS
Coal Chamber
NAILGUN

BOBBY PULEO
NOSEGRIND / OGDEN

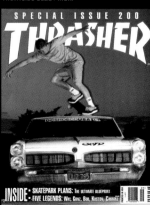

SPECIAL ISSUE 200

INSIDE • SKATEPARK PLANS: THE ULTIMATE BLUEPRINT
• FIVE LEGENDS: Way, Gonz, Bob, Koston, Carroll

DANNY WAY
BACKSIDE NOSEBLUNT SLIDE / OGDEN

INSIDE:
Biggest Air Ever
DWARVES
Chad Knight
RAMPAGE
X-Crement
LA DONNAS
Tucson

KEITH HUFNAGEL
OLLIE / MORF

JEREMY WRAY
OIL TANK GAP OLLIE / STURT

TEXAS PIPES
Demolition
US Bombs
Lurkage
Ozzy

BRIAN ANDERSON
TAILSLIDE / MORF

OGDEN

1997

NINETY-SEVEN STARTS with an epic mini-ramp battle at new dad Thiebaud's in Oakland. Screw 32 blaze tunes while Cardiel attempts backflips during the Death Match. Pier 7 is in effect. Eric Koston claims SOTY honors, following a retrospective of would-be winners from clay wheel days. Phares rules 'Rosa, Kit Erikson leaves Earth and is remembered at the Maritime Hall. Mike Maldonado backside 180s Sabin Alley on the steep slope of California Street. James Kelch talks football. Tim McKenney talks Beta Carotene. Cardiel loses skin for one of the sickest all-time Indy ads. The mag celebrates 200 issues and unleashes plans for the Warlord park, built in Your Town, USA. Sturt poaches the biggest air ever, beating the rest of the world to the newsstand with photos of Danny Way's heli-drops and subsequent blasts. Bob, Way, Koston, Carroll, and Gonz set it straight. X Games get served. Consolidated calls out Nike. Everything is bigger in Texas, including the fullpipes. Ozzy lives.

Max Schaaf skated for himself in his mom's house—indoors, vert, style. Schax

Potrero Hill varial heel by the little pony, **Bobby Puleo**

THREAD
THE NEEDLE

THIS RAIL IS BY MY HOUSE on Potrero Hill. It's steep, fast as hell, kinked, and a lot closer to that tree than it looks. It's a boardslide for a goofy-footer. I thought Gonz, then called Cards—he was down for it. After three tries he looked at me and asked, "Is it a make?" I said "Yeah," and

"THEN IT GOT UGLY... FORTY-FIVE ATTEMPTS, 35 WIPEOUTS, ONE KO."

then it got ugly… Forty-five attempts, 35 wipeouts, one KO. Luke shot this photo

of his face when he was lying on the ground. We made a mock cover out of it but the publisher pulled it: "Just a little too gnarly." The spot is gone now. Nobody else ever even tried.
—*Jake Phelps*

JAMES KELCH REVISITED … BEST HELLRIDE OF ALL TIME, PHIL SHAO SINGLE-HANDEDLY TERMINATES EUROPE … AMMO GETS BLOWN OUT BY CARDIEL, WHO GOES UP TO 10:30 IN THE 24-FOOT PIPE OF THE GODS …

Mike York front crooks the New Spot; EMB was gone, but never forgotten

Peter Hewitt when he was still riding for a bong company

Below: After 22 days on the road, **Cards** was still down to scare the troops

The oldest park in Madrid gets murdered by **JC**. Weeds on the deck, no flat—we thought we ripped it 'til we saw video of Hosoi doing 540s there

Opposite page: **Kareem Campbell**, ollie to fakie. Who is that on the right?

OGDEN

"IT'S BARGE ALL THE WAY. JUDGEMENT DAY, DECEMBER 1997"

"A GUY SAYING SOMETHING YOU MIGHT WANT TO HEAR"

LEGEND:
ERIC KOSTON

By RICK HOWARD

IT'S KIND OF LAME, right? That Eric talks to himself as much as he does? I mean, it's obvious he's a guy saying something you might want to hear. What's on his mind and what's he saying? Not sure, but apparently he's his own best advisor and those 40-minute pep talks he gives himself are still setting him apart from anyone else. Put 'em all on audiotape, Koston. We'll buy the box set.

Rails, stairs, hubbas, and indoor bowls, **Koston** can really do it all

BURNETT

POACHED!

THE SCOOP OF
THE YEAR

WHEN THE DC CREW decided to build a spot for Danny Way to do some monster air, it was a closed event—but that didn't stop commando Dan Sturt from poaching the shot. Sealed in an oil drum and delivered to the airport under the noses of the best in the business, Sturt got the photos. Our mag was going to press that following week; his images came to me, we planned accordingly,

"REKINDLED THE AGE OLD TWS VERSUS THRASHER WARS"

and off it went to be printed. By the time everyone found out, we had even beaten their DC ads to press. Lots of "phone calls" and "sorries," but hey, the scoop is where we become "journalists" and not "hacks."

End result: Danny Way heli-drop in Mexico, Sturt banned from everywhere, and the age-old TWS versus *Thrasher* wars are rekindled. So sick. —*Jake Phelps*

What's funny about this 5-0 on the bar in Madrid? He's like six walls in, he ollied both channels, had a back lip, and a 5-0 on the top rope. **Phil Shao** was all up in this shit. Miss you, blood

... KOSTON'S SOTY: "THANKS, I GUESS" ... EQUADOR HAS A PIPE WHERE YOU CAN GET STABBED WHILE DOWNING ENOUGH SHRIMP AND CERVEZA TO KILL AN ARMY ... TONY HAWK GETS WORKED LIPSLIDING A 10-STAIR

1998

"My friends are gonna be there, too."
—*Bon Scott*

"EL DIABLE ESTA PERDIDO"
ARTWORK BY PUSHEAD

PAT DUFFY
KICKFLIP / OGDEN

PETER HEWITT
FRONTSIDE INVERT / OGDEN

BOB BURNQUIST
OLLIE / OGDEN

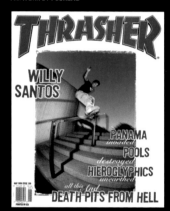

WILLY SANTOS
FRONTSIDE FEEBLE / BURNETT

MIKE CARROLL
FRONTSIDE CROOKED GRIND / MORF

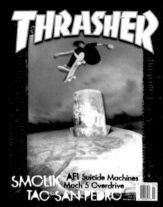

ETHAN FOWLER
360 FLIP / MORF

BAM MARGERA
OVER VERT GRIND / OGDEN

MARC JOHNSON
SWITCH FRONTSIDE HEELFLIP / MORF

WADE SPEYER AND DAEWON SONG
PORTRAITS / OGDEN

JOHN CARDIEL
FRONTSIDE AIR / MORF

CAIRO FOSTER
CROOKED GRIND / OGDEN

1998

PUSHEAD STARTS OFF the year with a psychedelic zombie of a crooked grind. The Hellriders head to Lima and Quito, noted with Peter Hewitt's frontal on top of 13 feet. Bob Gnar is SOTY. The cement parks continue to sprout: Ethan with a tré over a trash can at Petaluma, and an innocently fresh-faced Bam Margera at FDR. A-Team are the techest of the tech, and Marc Johnson reps it with a South Bay switch frontside heelflip over a fence and gap. Fu Manchu. AFI. Scribble Jam. Two of the best covers ever are consecutive: Daewon and Wade posing as poster boys for fresh and hesh, followed by Cardiel's head-high, boned, ramp-to-ramp transfer over some paint cans in the rain. There's an indoor square pool two blocks from the office. The Butcher, Cairo, and Adrian Lopez arrive. Phil Shao, RIP.

True NorCal barbarian **Wade Speyer**: Chain wallet + method + Burnside = Droppin' bombs

BOB'S SOTY, THEN BACK TO BRAZIL … BASTIEN SALABANZI, AGE ELEVEN … THE GRUMPIES GET NAKED… BENEFIT FOR RUBEN ORKIN, WHO'S DIAGNOSED WITH CANCER … JEREMY WRAY: TALLEST 50-50 OF ALL TIME …

Already recognized as money, **Marc Johnson** fried brain cells with a nosegrind nollie heel out. Sold lots of shoes

Early radar of coming insanity, **Bastien Salabanzi** back Smiths a waist-high (to him) bench in the French

Below: Road Dogs are hard to find and harder to keep. **HRC** C-Bowl, 1998

Team Pierre and **Phil Shao**. NorCal starts in Palo Alto

Black and blue and back for more, **Erik Ellington** mans up

"STILL THE MOST PUNK AND TALENTED AND FREE"

LEGEND: BOB BURNQUIST

By MAX SCHAAF

Early morning Marseilles juice, **Bob** rides the pigeon to hell

THE FIRST TIME I heard of Bob was when the Anti-Hero guys got back from a Brazil trip with Jake. Let me preface this by saying Jake would regularly come to me with people's names like Joe Blow, and say, "They're the best. This guy is taking over vert." I remember Jake saying, "I got two words for you, Max, 'Brian Patch'." It was his way of saying you better stay up on your game. I was skating vert everyday at the time, so he knew I would care if there was some dude I'd never heard of about to take over. Brian Patch never took over vert. Thanks for that one, Jake.

Anyway, Jake and these guys get back from Brazil, and Jake is like, "Bob! Bob! Bob!" He was telling me about the things Bob was doing, and it was tough as shit. Jake told me Bob could switch backside roll-in into anything. That's fucking hard. So I could imagine this Brazilian skater named Bob was pretty rad—but because Jake was telling the story I didn't really buy it all the way. So some months later Jake calls and says, "Bob is here from Brazil and Ruben is going to take him over to your ramp." It was funny, because there were actually some other pro skaters skating my ramp that day; I think it was Crum,

Hendrix, and maybe the Pappas bros. I look over my shoulder and Ruben and this lanky kid, barefoot with his shoes hanging from his neck, walk back to my ramp. I think to myself, "Well, this must be BOB." He walks up, Ruben introduces us, and I meet Bob Burnquist.

So he puts his gear on and drops in, and his first run was hairball to say the least. His arms were everywhere; he was all over the place, but it was rad. I remember telling him to watch out for the beam. At the time my ramp had a beam on the platform that you'd smack your head on if you went up the wrong spot. So, of course, his next run he goes to do a frontside blunt and goes right into it—I mean he cracks his head into the beam, knocking all this dust and shit onto the ramp. I was like, "Whoa! Bob ain't so bright." Later I learned he was just super nervous (anyone who knows Bob now knows he is seldom nervous). The session ends, I say "Later," and tell him to call if he wants to skate again.

He ends up staying in SF for a bit, and we skate together a bunch. I quickly learned Bob is one of the most talented vert skaters there is. As soon as it was just him and me skating and he was relaxed,

he blazed. This was like 10 years ago and he did backside noseblunt reverts, switch backside roll-ins, switch back lips—it goes on and on. The best thing about it was, after skating, Bob would go out into The City with Rube and the boys and party it up; get wasted, do the stuff, and still come over and kill it the next day. At the time, vert skaters were kind of robotic and drinking weird power drinks, but Bob, who looked like a dirtbag, was getting shit-faced at night so it was kind of a breath of fresh air.

Then Bob went home to Brazil for a bit and was planning on moving back to the States. He comes back, wins Slam City Jam, gets on Anti-Hero, and just starts killing it. People were shocked. It was awesome. This guy from nowhere comes out doing shit on a skateboard that people had only dreamed of. He had, like, two sponsors and was wearing some stretched out T-shirt and cutoffs with holes in them. I remember thinking, "This is great, Bob's our friend. He's not like all those other dudes. He's gonna change this thing."

Bob ended up living at my house for a while. We skated a bunch and had some good times. There were some serious sessions with the two of us by ourselves, just rapid progression. But he was on a whole other kick! He was learning so fast. Bob turned pro for Anti-Hero and started traveling a bunch, winning contests, and making a name for himself. I remember I started seeing Bob get more wrapped in himself and money and his image, which is natural, but I fucking loved the underground Bob. One day he told me, "I want to be famous like Tony Hawk."

I remember being like, "Fuck that. You're Bob. Be who you are." This was kind of where my relationship with Bob started to fade, because to me I had never seen someone so punk and talented and free as Bob, so I couldn't figure why he wanted to be like someone else. I thought Bob would be the dude that won the contest, had a $10,000 bill in one hand and a bottle of Jim Beam in the other, and then make some outrageous comment on the mic and maybe put Don Bostick in a headlock. Wouldn't that be rad?

Funny thing, though: one thing that's never changed about Bob is that he is still the most punk and talented and free when he skateboards. I can't stand watching the X Games; all those jocks with their gold chains and their energy drink sponsors doing some hip-hop thing with their hands as they walk off the ramp. But I *have* to watch. I mute the TV and I wait for Bob to skate. It's still that same dude who showed up at my ramp over 10 years ago, arms everywhere and all over the place—and so fucking rad. I watch with a book or magazine so that as soon as he's done I can cover my face and edit runs myself.

That's how I came to know Bob.

Mark Scott did more for skating than anyone you will ever know. Seventies trick (Elguerial), '90s spot (Burnside), forever dude (Red). When Red rides Burnside, he rides alone

RED AND MARTY. THE MONUMENTS THESE DUDES HAVE BUILT WILL BE ON EARTH FOREVER.
PHOTO: MARTINEAU

BURNSIDE

WHEN THEY FIRST STARTED digging and piling dirt up against that wall, that bridge, the energy was so high— so powerful—because no one knew or had any idea what it was going to become. It was such a living-in-the-present, "What are you going to do today?" work towards the unknown future. But it knew, that wall knew; and everybody could feel it and everybody came. We were drawn by the independence of the project; it became the king of gnar. If you were gnar you moved there and lived there and tried to out-do the first resident of the park, who was Germ. He lived under a quarterpipe cavern tunnel and had a baby under there, and skated and worked, puked, and got fucked up. And it goes on. Everyday, whether you're there or not, it's going off right now.

"NO ONE COULD HAVE KNOWN HOW FAR THIS WOULD GO."

The outcome inspired a whole new era of skater-builders, taking architecture to the next level, building whatever they wanted and not caring if anyone came to ride it or not. Come to help, and you're in. That inspired a new kind of camaraderie that has taken this inspiration further than we ever dreamed, because the energy among us is amplified through these structures. The input, the belonging— we are all pushing the pedal through the floor boards 'cause there's no speed limit. There's no end.

But it has begun, and the momentum is pushing across the world into a manifestation, a concrete conformation, nation by nation in liberation. Seeds that were sewn have grown many homes. No one could have known how far this would go. —*Monk*

MORF

LUKE
OGDEN

I'VE KNOW HIM SINCE 1984. He was some little kid who was sitting next to me on my way to Joe Lopes' ramp. He was like 14. I was already wise to the skate grub lifestyle, and I could tell he was quite uncomfortable sitting there. Quiet and introverted he is; loud and obnoxious I am.

"WE'VE FOUGHT, SPIT AND BRAWLED OUR WAY INTO THE MAG"

We used to work at the same skateshop in the mid '80s setting up decks and heckling kids. In 1996 there was a meltdown at the plant: the art director and photo editor left in the same week. I needed someone fast. I called Luke and he was in.

After I set the tone, we took the car for a joyride. We went everywhere and skated everything. We've fought, spit, and brawled our way into the mag. For all his lack of communication skills, he's an amazing photographer. I call him my friend, my bro, and he can kinda skate. Best trip for Luke and me: America '99 with Windy and Curtis. —*Jake Phelps*

Brian Anderson came to California from Connecticut to get some, and he got: SOTY, slot on Toy Machine, and some snaps over a college rail

... WARNER MOB GETS THE JUICE ... EVERYONE WANTS THE DONNAS ... ED COLVER GETS THE RECOGNITION HE DESERVES ... MUSKA SPINS (RECORDS) ... ELISSA STEAMER SHOWS THE GIRLS HOW TO GET SOME

OGDEN

BURNETT

Young Spawn **Dustin Dollin** had many moods

Left: **Cardiel** smoked the C-Bowl in Cambridge, MA. Forevs spot, awesome dude. Brutal display of power, madness, and loneliness

THE LETTER CARRIERS sure get a kick outta these bombs. Check out some of the greats. Often times the envelopes are empty, so when you send yours in tell a story, too. And quit biting the shots in the mag

1999

"There aren't any crazy sluts
at the demos I go to."
—*Andrew Reynolds*

GIRLS WHO RIP • SICK NEW PARKS • KILLER PHOTOS

THRASHER

Interviews
CAIRO FOSTER
JEREMY KLEIN
GIORGIO ZATTONI

Tunes
BLACK STAR
FURY 66
BERZERK

RICHARD MULDER
SWITCH OLLIE / BURNETT

NEW YORK • GONZ • SUPERMODELS • ALVA • AUSTRALIA

THRASHER

JOE PINO
JUMPS FROM AN AIRPLANE

BOB BURNQUIST
GOES THROUGH THE ROOF

JETS TO BRAZIL
BREAKS YOUR JAW

GEOFF ROWLEY
FRONTSIDE BOARDSLIDE / STURT

WEST • HILL • GONZ • McCRANK • GETZ • SENN • PAEZ • FOSTER

THRASHER

COAST to COAST
DESTRUCTION

RICK HOWARD
CROOKED GRIND / OGDEN

ANDREW REYNOLDS • SKATER OF THE YEAR 1998

THRASHER

ANDREW REYNOLDS
FRONTSIDE BLUNTSLIDE / DIGGS

AGNOSTIC FRONT • RICKY OYOLA JAILED IN OZ

THRASHER

EMB
Rest in Peace

JAPAN
Hassle Free

AROUND THE WORLD
in 19 days

JERRY HSU
SWITCH HEELFLIP / MORF

GERSHON DESTROYS TAMPA

THRASHER

GBH
PUNK AND PROUD

ARIZONA
PARKS AND POOLS

ROCKY
PUMPED AND PSYCHOTIC

JEFF LENOCE
5-0 / STEWART

DONNY BARLEY • INTERVIEWS • TONY TRUJILLO

THRASHER

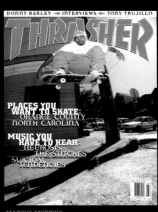

PLACES YOU WANT TO SKATE:
ORANGE COUNTY
NORTH CAROLINA

MUSIC YOU HAVE TO HEAR:
NEUROSIS
THE STITCHES
SUICIDAL TENDENCIES

MARCUS McBRIDE
OLLIE / OGDEN

JAMIE THOMAS • HAMMERHEAD ATTACK!!

THRASHER

JAMIE THOMAS
SWITCH FRONTSIDE LIPSLIDE / BURNETT

FREE PULL-OUT POSTER • PURE SKATE POWER

THRASHER

INTERVIEWS
ROWLEY
SUMNER
NEW PARKS
ANNIHILATION

ROYCE NELSON
TRANSFER / OGDEN

CREAGER QUESTS • DYLLA SPEAKS • ANDERSON CONQUERS

THRASHER

ROAD TRIP FEVER USA

ROLL THROUGH EUROPE

NEW JERSEY
MASSACHUSETTS
TEXAS
ARIZONA
NEW MEXICO
ALABAMA
COLORADO
NORTH CAROLINA

ENGLAND
GERMANY
SCOTLAND
HOLLAND
SWEDEN
DENMARK

KERRY GETZ
KICKFLIP LIEN AIR / BURNETT

YOUNG GUNS: RYAN JOHNSON AND KRISTIAN SVITAK

THRASHER

YOUTH GONE MAD

RICHARD PAEZ
ALLEY-OOP NOLLIE / FREITAS

PHILADELPHIA • INLAND EMPIRE • NEW YORK • ARIZONA

THRASHER

LINCOLN CITY:
AMERICA'S GNARLIEST SKATEPARK

MARK SCOTT
FRONTSIDE AIR / OGDEN

Daniel Harold Sturt © 1999

1999

GEOFF ROWLEY frontside boardslides a 16-star over the lens of Sturt. Two pages later, Bob floats through the rafters of Andy's ramp in Oakland. NYC is alright, if you like saxophones. Andrew Reynolds, Florida's favorite son, is SOTY. The next issue, Jerry Hsu is christened Tech-Gnar. *Thrasher* Japan is more than just a magazine. A sign of the coming apocalypse, bulldozers clear the history from Justin Herman Plaza. In the distance, Richard Kirby takes it back to the Earth. At the same time, down Third Street a couple miles the New Spot is born. Mike Burnett introduces us to Rocky Norton, the poster boy for hold-everything big drops and burly lines. Jamie Thomas returns to The Bible. A bunch of Hosoi Hammerheads are pressed and handed out for some new takes on an old legend. Ryan Johnson, Kristian Svitak, Donny Barley, and Tony Trujillo are the young guns of the moment. Epic 'Crete continues to cure, documented in Royce Nelson's Alameda blast over the SF skyline and in Red's masterpiece, the gnarliest park in America, Lincoln City.

Geoff Rowley knows where to find the juice, and when he came *Thrasher*'s way we were happy to see him jump. Thanks Sturt

Opposite page: Lincoln City, OR, has the highest suicide rate in America, but why kill yourself when you can front rock like **Brian Seber** at the local skatepit?

Eric J is as underrated as they get. Ripper, loser, fucked; it all adds up to switch roll-ins into 10-foot-deep pools

No more running around in his undies at midnight. **Cairo Foster**; front nose this, bitch

"Dead men tell no tales." **Tim Brauch** was a class act and we miss him daily

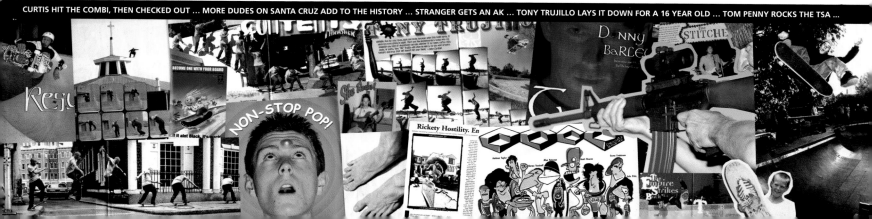

CURTIS HIT THE COMBI, THEN CHECKED OUT … MORE DUDES ON SANTA CRUZ ADD TO THE HISTORY … STRANGER GETS AN AK … TONY TRUJILLO LAYS IT DOWN FOR A 16 YEAR OLD … TOM PENNY ROCKS THE TSA …

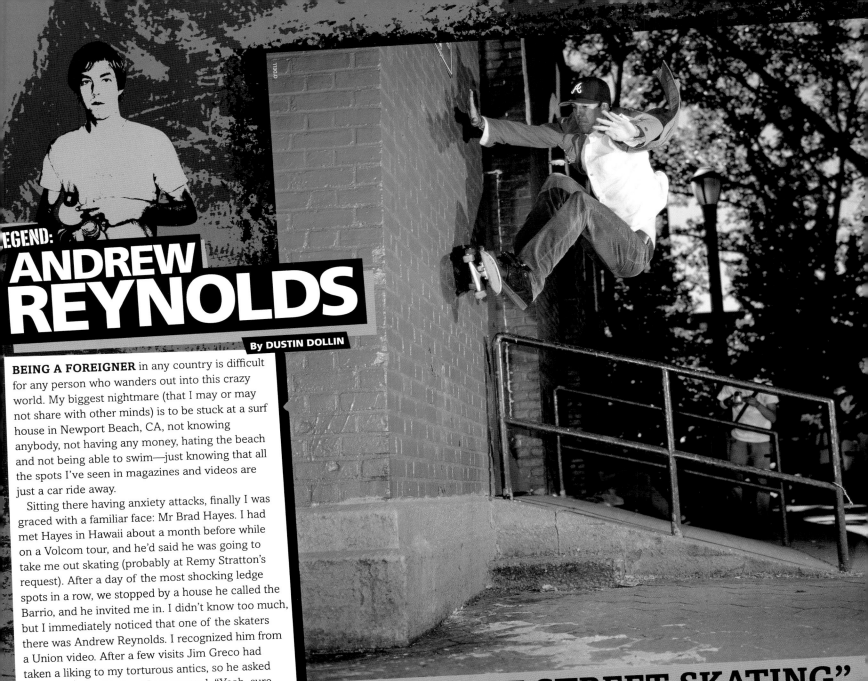

LEGEND:
ANDREW REYNOLDS

By DUSTIN DOLLIN

"THE BOSS OF STREET SKATING"

BEING A FOREIGNER in any country is difficult for any person who wanders out into this crazy world. My biggest nightmare (that I may or may not share with other minds) is to be stuck at a surf house in Newport Beach, CA, not knowing anybody, not having any money, hating the beach and not being able to swim—just knowing that all the spots I've seen in magazines and videos are just a car ride away.

Sitting there having anxiety attacks, finally I was graced with a familiar face: Mr Brad Hayes. I had met Hayes in Hawaii about a month before while on a Volcom tour, and he'd said he was going to take me out skating (probably at Remy Stratton's request). After a day of the most shocking ledge spots in a row, we stopped by a house he called the Barrio, and he invited me in. I didn't know too much, but I immediately noticed that one of the skaters there was Andrew Reynolds. I recognized him from a Union video. After a few visits Jim Greco had taken a liking to my torturous antics, so he asked Andrew if I could stay. He answered, "Yeah, sure, just don't try and stay here for too long."

After a couple of weeks Andrew did not get angry about me staying. He started buying me lunch and teaching me his ideas about how he thought skating should be. Thinking back, I can't believe how genuine and real Andrew was—and still is—with me and anybody else who had the pleasure to be in his immediate vicinity. This unique human was molded from the thousand ghosts of heaven and has been blessed with iron heels, incomparable skills, and the balls and motivation to keep pushing the limits of skateboarding so far past any of our wildest dreams.

I wonder if I should take out his knees and make it easier on every professional, amateur, dreamer, perpetrator, sell-out, buy-in, and shocker that tries to get in this industry, because this is the only way that any of us are going to be able to stop him.

Otherwise, he is going to continue to blow our minds. Even when Reynolds was a wreck, party-going maniac—that's right kids, even Reynolds has slept in the streets, been on the corner, crashed cars, and taken it as far as the body allows—he continued to blast out part after part of no-bullshit, pure street skating.

He and a small circle of other pros, who are probably featured in this book, are the reason for what skateboarding is today. Fuck what you hear or see on TV. I'd personally like to thank him for always counting me in when a lot of other people would have left me to rot. During those wonderful Piss Drunk times when none of the crew would have any money, Andrew (if he wasn't hung-over and felt like drinking himself) would be the first to offer product,

new or used, for us to go slang. Or even throw the BBQ or party on his own dime, 'cause that's what type of smooth motherfucker this guy is.

I don't know if it was his nice upbringing or just pure genetics that created this personality, but whatever it is, this guy has moved himself in the right direction of creating one of the most memorable skaters to bless this otherwise cold industry. Coming in hot, keeping it cool, and keeping it positive from the day he was born 'til the day he dies, this is the boss of street skating. Andrew Reynolds, we thank you. (PS: I want my frontside flip back. PPS: Slow the fuck down.)

What more needs to be said? The Boss—not Springsteen, just **Reynolds**—straight wall-jammin'

Colt Cannon back tails some popular bar in SF. Photo: Ogden

UP ON THEM BARS

When Pat Duffy grinded the gigantic double kink in Plan B's 1991 *Questionable* video, a skate population who started their four-wheeled adventure on pool coping or flying off launch ramps threw up their hands in dismay at the incredible magic of it all. Not so for the skaters of the 2000's. For them, the flat bar is their driveway kicker and the round-bar 50-50

"A NEW RANK OF PROFESSIONAL HANDRAIL MANIACS"

is a skill acquired in the same amount of time it took the previous generation to grunt their way through that first Russian boneless—approximately six to 16 months. Two-thousand saw the reign of the gigantic 50-50, which purists quickly dismissed as "not that hard," but soon the rail tricks became not only big, but big *and* tech. Entering a world where 360 flip lips and back tail shove-its are standard fare, today's skater follows only one rule: if you can do it on a flat bar, you can do it down a handrail. That mantra, coupled with the proliferation of skatepark "training" rails, has produced an explosion of formerly unheard of maneuvers, including Chris Haslam's kickflip backside Smith and Chris Cole's kickflip backside noseblunt and a new rank of professional handrail maniacs. It has also produced a scary trend of under-skilled daredevils throwing themselves off 20-plus stair cliffs like lemmings. Be careful kids, and please use the rail. —*Michael Burnett*

Toronto Terror **Mark Appleyard**, switch crooks. Butteryard means smooth
Opposite page: **The Butcher** floats one while thinking about the future, his wife, and Argentina. Chop chop, baby. Visalia

... MARSY ONE HAPPENS, THE BEST OF THE BEST: WIRE TO WIRE WADE SPEYER ... ROWLEY & THOMAS IN ONE YEAR? I'D SAY WE WERE DOING ALRIGHT

2000

"School just rubbed me
the wrong way."
—*Matt Mumford*

SPECIAL COLLECTOR'S EDITION · TONY HAWK'S 900°

THRASHER

GREATS:
CAB
GONZ
HOSOI
BLENDER
REYNOLDS

HIGH AIR:
WAY
UEDA
BURNQUIST

TRIPLE
KOSTON
ROWLEY
McCRANK

STEVE CABALLERO
FRONTSIDE AIR / THATCHER

ARIZONA · MINNESOTA · OREGON · NEBRASKA

THRASHER

KILLER SPOTS
Hella parks
Auto rails
Secret pools

ERIK ELLINGTON
BACKSIDE FLIP / BURNETT

GANG STARR · JOE STRUMMER · EAST COAST RIPPERS

THRASHER

INSIDE: MUMFORD
URUGUAY BRAZIL
CHILE CHALMERS
ARGENTINA
DISOBEDIENCE

PAUL MACHNAU
FRONTSIDE SLIDER / BURNETT

SKATER OF THE YEAR 1999 · BRIAN ANDERSON

THRASHER

BRIAN ANDERSON
MORF, OGDEN

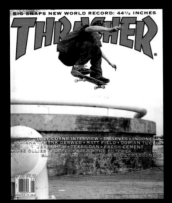

BIG SNAPS NEW WORLD RECORD: 44½ INCHES

THRASHER

REESE FORBES
FAKIE OLLIE / OGDEN

SOUL BRAINS · WORLDWIDE SKATE COVERAGE

THRASHER

LONDON

GRECO

PETERSEN

TEMPLETON

JAPAN

CRO-MAGS

DENNIS BUSENITZ
OLLIE / OGDEN

ARTO SAARI · THE SICKEST PHOTOS EVER

THRASHER

ARTO SAARI
CROOKED GRIND / STURT

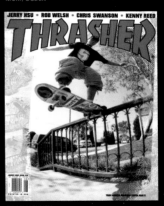

JERRY HSU · ROB WELSH · CHRIS SWANSON · KENNY REED

THRASHER

TOAN NGUYEN
KICKFLIP BACK TAIL / BURNETT

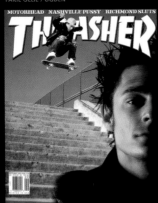

MOTORHEAD · NASHVILLE PUSSY · RICHMOND SLUTS

THRASHER

JIM GRECO
SWITCH FRONTSIDE FLIP / OGDEN

DE LA SOUL · CIVIC MINDED 5 · BOY SETS FIRE

THRASHER

HOT SPOTS:
NeW YoRK
eSPaNa
PHilaDeLPHia
BoSToN

HOT SHOTS:
MuSKa
SMoLiK
KaLiS Getz

CAIRO FOSTER
FRONTSIDE NOSESLIDE / OGDEN

KITTIE · THE EXPLOSION · SCRIBBLE JAM

THRASHER

INSIDE:
UNDERGROUND
PIPES
TONY HAWK
X-GAMES
HEADS:
STACY LOWERY
PAT WASHINGTON
AARON SUSKI
DAXTER LUSSIER

JASON DILL
BLUNTSLIDE / DAWES

FOREIGN LEGION · PUNK ROCK ON THE ROAD · KING DIAMOND

THRASHER

JAPAN · TORONTO
Brandon Biebel · Chad Knight · Steve Bailey
FROGFACE

ERIC KOSTON
BACKSIDE LIPSLIDE / BURNETT

2000

KOSTON STARTS the year with a nollie heel nose at ARCO, the first done on a rail. Vinny Vegas busts his best trick as an unknown. Apples gets on Circa with a massive switch tail ad. Biebel crosses over to Girl and Lakai. Websites MonsterSkate.com and HardCloud.com promise to change how we skate the Web with two-page ads. Bucky gets a disease and a new shoe sponsor in the Genetic ads. Fabrizio Santos is the latest Brazilian terror. Adam Louder hardflips to back lip a rail. Lindsey Robertson gets his first photo. Pat Washington barely has time to skate he's getting so many record offers. Shorty's is hot, Stevie gets his DC shoe, Greco switch frontside flips Lincoln on the edge of addiction. Hsu busts for Maple, the Osiris D3 is a best seller. Rich Cooley dominates all wack ads. Trainwreck makes a brief appearance. New bucks: Appleyard, Danny Garcia, Chris Dobstaff, Toan Nguyen, Trainwreck, Jake Nunn. How to quit skating. Mike V fights jock ethics by jumping trash cans in Oakley blades. BA celebrates his 1999 SOTY status with a ghetto fab cover. Mumford makes his *Thrasher* debut. Lopez takes the rail front blunt to the highest level. Ellington gets his first cover. The world didn't end. Anatomy gets invented and the arrows always know. Geoff Rowley wraps up the year with the big SOTY award.

Brandon Biebel made it out of the Sixteen clique, tried Expedition, and ended up on Girl. Holla at the switch heel

Opposite page: Huntington Beach sucks. Stranger and I got escorted off the contest site 'cause we were yelling for **Tony**… Tony said "Fuck it" and jumped into the flat bank

DREADS ARE COOL … TOO SHORT REPS ECKO … COLE, BEFORE THE EAGLE GOT HIM … CAIRO, PROPER FORM ON THE RIBBON THREE FLIP … GREG CARROLL TOUGH GUY WALK THROUGH …

Peter Hewitt, frontside invert over Crested Butte, CO. In space, no one can hear you scream

Cards signs his Spitfire ad. Only he knows how to spell "gnarly"

Arto and **Geoff** tag-teamed the same rail. Here, Arto back noseblunts. These two dudes scared everyone

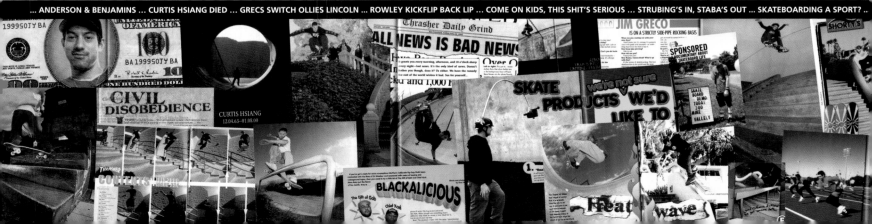

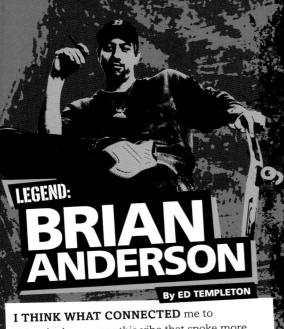

LEGEND:
BRIAN ANDERSON

By ED TEMPLETON

I THINK WHAT CONNECTED me to Brian Anderson was this vibe that spoke more of my generation of skaters than the one he was existing in. He was just skating for fun, and there truly was nothing else to it. No dreams of getting sponsored and going pro—and that's what made him very different. Brian was on the West Coast staying with some people in SF, CA, or maybe Sacto, CA, when the Toy team of the time was in NorCal filming for *Welcome to Hell*.

Since he grew up skating with Donny Barley, we hooked up and brought him out with us. The moment came when he manhandled this handicap rail at SF State. He was so big! Just a beast of a dude, and he acted so on a skateboard. The kind of stuff that most people freak out about was nothing to him. Chad Muska and I just looked at each other and we knew we wanted him on the team. He was sketchy, but we loved it, and could see past it. Later he gave us some footage that he had because he was living with skater-filmer Mike Rafter. The shot of him rolling up to the Hubba Hideout with a Bic'ed head and a pissed face sent shivers through all who watched it. You knew damage was going down. Front blunt? No problem.

Once he got on he began filming for the video with Jamie Thomas, who would constantly call me with a new story about the biggest thing ever done by BA. He was ruling San Diego, CA. He flew past the rest of the people on the team as far as being a deserving pro. Even the guys who were on before him had to admit that he was the one who should go first—but they could only admit that because he was the real deal. Everyone knew it, and he was not cocky about it in the slightest. Then I remember sitting in my living room with him talking about turning professional. Instead of saying, "Hell yeah! Where's my check?" he said he wasn't sure if that was what he wanted. Now that was shocking! I was like, "Man, this is free money!" But he wasn't sure if the responsibility was one he wanted to take on. He didn't want to *have* to skate. He had dreams

BA the barbarian front blunts in Oz. Looks like a trophy, don't it?

of going to school to become a chef and settling down somewhere. I had to admire that; number one, his realization that it could kill the fun of skating for him, and number two, having a real head on his shoulders. I told him at the very least he should use skating to save some money for the rest of his life. He agreed.

Once he decided to take it seriously, the change was incredible. He'd been to some contests before, but he just skated and didn't worry about doing well. After this mind set shift he went to Europe and cleaned up and then came home and cleaned up, crushing all who would dare in any contest he entered and taking the big prize money. It was amazing to see what someone with talent could do when they focused.

was the business. These simple facts are the things that add that extra greatness to anything I see of Brian. The combination of a giant man who looks unconceivable as a skateboarder gets on a board and he's the picture of grace and style. He skates with an inner soundtrack, grooving to the cracks and the curbs like dancing. He holds his airtime past possible, and like all the best skateboarders ever, you can tell just by watching them on flat that they have that special thing: the power at his disposal in that massive skeleton giving him a crushing capacity to amaze, snapping eight- and a half-inch decks like toothpicks and handling his board just as cunningly. All this, and having never wanted anything else but to cook food for a living.

"THE MAN WHO TRIPPED AND BECAME FAMOUS"

When his skate duties were over, he would take a trip to Europe alone to erase the whole skate world from his head. I feel like being around the skate industry side of things really takes a toll on him; the last thing he ever wanted to talk about

He treats professional skateboarding like the impostor that it is and keeps his mind firmly in reality, knowing that pro skating isn't. He is the man who tripped and became famous in this small world of ours.

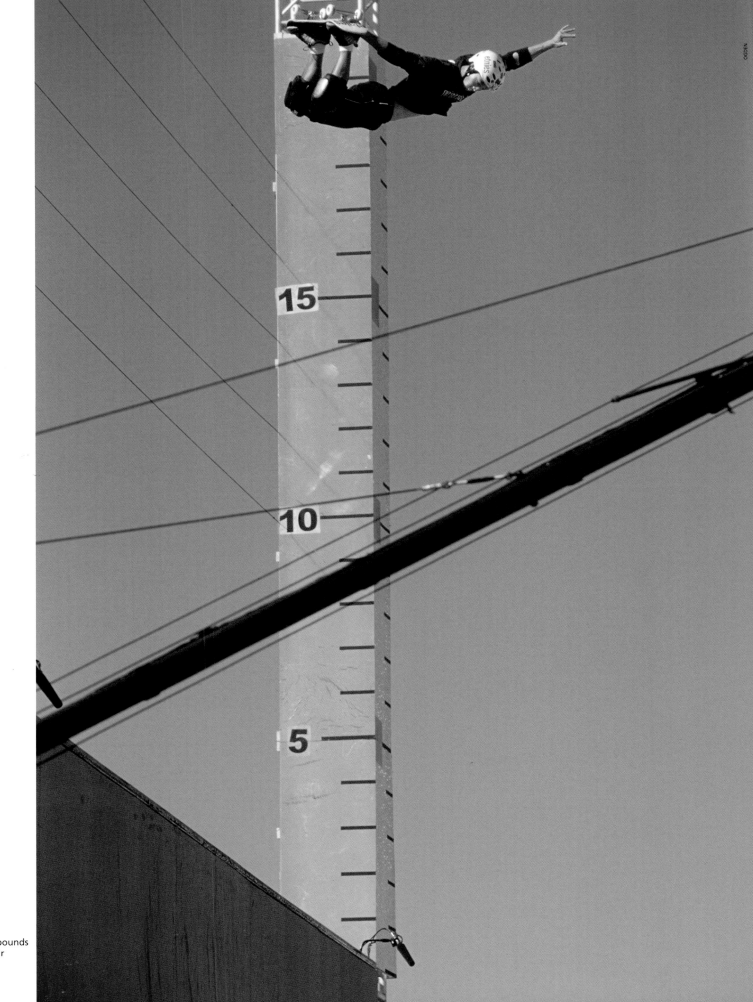

Lincoln Ueda goes
completely out-of-bounds
with this method air

John Janeway, way over your head. SF, CA

… CHALMERS HOOKS A STALEFISH … CAIRO SHOWS PURPLE … CARDS DOES THE LEVI'S RAIL IN STYLE … JEREME ROGERS LOOKS MIGHTY SMALL … THE VORTEX: A TRUE SKATER KILLER … MIKE CONROY, BACK ON RADAR

FROM VIDEOS, hats, and tunes to pentagram hoodies, *Thrasher* gear is only for the serious-minded schralpers. And it pays the bills

2001

"Technology will destroy all spirit of individuality."
—*Jake Phelps*

SPECIAL 244 PAGE COLLECTOR'S EDITION

THRASHER

TWENTIETH ANNIVERSARY

PENNY
GRECO
DILL
ALVA
STEAMER
BARLEY
HOWARD
REYNOLDS
BURNQUIST
TEMPLETON

KALIS
GETZ
DUFFY
McKAY
SHEFFEY
DREHOBL
McCRANK
MARIANO
BUCCHIERI
ELLINGTON

Twenty Years
And Grinding

ANONYMOUS
"PUSHING AHEAD" / OGDEN

INTERNATIONAL NOISE CONSPIRACY • MISSING 23½ • DEAD PREZ

THRASHER

TECH GNAR SUPERSTARS

JERON WILSON INTERVIEW

COOKIN' IN COLORADO

STEVE OLSON
SWITCH CROOKS / BURNETT

10 PAGES OF MARK APPLEYARD • NYC • HAWAII ROCKS • GURU

THRASHER

BEATDOWN
GRECO vs. ROWLEY

ANARCHY
DOWN UNDER

DREHOBL
ANDERSON
STABA and
UPSON

DESTROY
AUSTRALIA

DAN DREHOBL
FRONTSIDE AIR / OGDEN

GEOFF ROWLEY × SKATER of the YEAR

THRASHER

GEOFF ROWLEY
PORTRAIT / STURT

GONZ • MONTREAL • PIPES • SAMIAM • MEXICO

THRASHER

AM INVASION

ELIAS BINGHAM
BASTIEN SALABANZI
PATRICK MELCHER
JOEL MEINHOLZ
COLT CANNON
CHRIS COLE

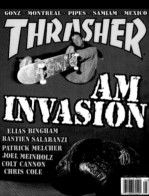

ELIAS BINGHAM
DEEP SHIFTY / OGDEN

SPECIAL ISSUE: OVER VERT AND BEYOND

THRASHER

TAMPA PRO
THE LOOP OF DEATH
WHO MADE IT. WHO GOT SERVED

SNOOP DOGG
SKATES G-FOOTED

JERRY HSU
HAS A POSSE

HAWAII
KALE IS CRAZY

ALAN PETERSEN
FRONTSIDE OLLIE / OGDEN

10 YEARS OF TEMPLETON

THRASHER

STEVIE
WILLIAMS
NO LUCK INVOLVED

AUSTRALIA

HEADSHOTS
MELCHER • PULEO • LENOCE

SICK SOUNDS

BIG GUNS
EL TORO 20
DESTROYED

STEVIE WILLIAMS
FRONTSIDE NOSESLIDE / WOODS

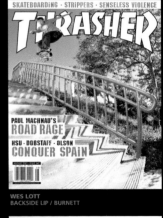

SKATEBOARDING • STRIPPERS • SENSELESS VIOLENCE

THRASHER

PAUL MACHNAU'S
ROAD RAGE

HSU • DOBSTAFF • OLSON
CONQUER SPAIN

WES LOTT
BACKSIDE LIP / BURNETT

INSANE 30 PAGE FLIP EURO TOUR BLOWOUT

THRASHER

ON THE ROAD
ROWLEY, BASTIEN
ARTO & APPLEYARD

ROCKERS
MURDER CITY DEVILS
ALKALINE TRIO
FUGAZI • XZIBIT • LARS

GEOFF ROWLEY
BACKSIDE 50-50 / BURNETT

SKATEBOARD MAGAZINE FROM HELL

THRASHER

ROAD DOGS
THOMAS
MUMFORD
ROWLEY

CHERRY PARK
LOWERY
MONTOYA

DEAD MAN SKATING
DREHOBL

ZOUNDS
WHITE STRIPES
UNWOUND ANTISEEN

MATT FIELD
FRONTSIDE NOSEGRIND / MORF

ISSUE 250 OF THE DARK AND GNARLY

THRASHER

1 OF 2
COLLECTABLE
COVERS

RYAN SMITH
READY TO BLOW

ERIC KOSTON
STANDS UP TALL

STACY LOWERY
THIS GUY IS HUGE

ALSO INSIDE
DENVER • BUILT TO SPILL TOYS THAT KILL
AMERICAN STEEL KANSAS CITY • CHICAGO
AUSTRIAN STRIP CLUBS & THE RUSSIAN MOB

MARK APPLEYARD
FRONT SMITH / BURNETT

BAKER ON TOUR: AMS GO NUTS THESE KIDS ARE NOT ALRIGHT...

THRASHER

DISCOVERED:
THE LOST
SKATEPARK

RIPDOGS:
CHAD FERNANDEZ
CASWELL BERRY
PETER SMOLIK

STEVE BAILEY
FRONTSIDE OLLIE / OGDEN

2001

OUR 20TH ANNIVERSARY is a who's who of boarding's best—includes the last documented Sean Sheffey skate photos. Colt Cannon wins Tampa just ahead of Bastien, Chris Cole, and Corey Duffel. Dustin Charlton gets hit in the head with a toilet, Ryan Smith blows up. Jon Allie makes the mag with a noseblunt down 10 while Koston noseslides the giant curved rail at Philly's city hall. Lil' Evan Hernandez front boards the big 18 for a Baker ad. Flip owns the September mag with a 30-page Euro article and Geoff's ultra-gnar gap to 50-50 cover on the massive Lyon hubba. Appleyard takes the pro plunge. Cherry Park is the best place to skate and cause drama in the LBC, Dan Drehobl opens a coffin, Caswell Berry cuts his pony tail and makes the mag, Colt Cannon kickflips to nose on Clipper, and Anthony Mosely back tails it to fakie. Keenan Milton RIP. Ellington jumps from Zero to Baker and back unscathed. Lance Mountain Jr ushers in the scumstache revival. Savier footwear temporarily bump Brad Staba to a higher tax bracket. Machnau mangles all rails, Rob Dyrdek grinds a 20—after the rail gets switched from round to square and the TV cameras are rolling for DC's prime time debut. Terry Kennedy tries the Opera House rail and gets got. Don Nguyen ollies El Toro but we call him "Dan." Stevie Williams gets the cover and Ed Templeton gets a career retrospective and dips into his gnar reserves to lipslide the big 18. We promise Snoop Dogg the cover but bury him in the back. The loop at Tampa Pro almost murders several, including SPOT's Brian Schaeffer. Natural Koncept finally gets their Hawaii tour article and Choppy doesn't sleep the whole week. Cardiel grinds the massive Union Square rail, hesh starts to outpace fresh, and Arto Saari is named Skater of the Year.

FREITAS

Classic **Jason Jessee** is all we can say about this ollie

Opposite page: **Diego Bucchieri** waited two weeks to get this double set; he had to run and jump on his board, snap, and hope. He actually bent his axle on the make. This shit is burl-school

OZ IS STILL COOL WITH STRANGER AND CORPSY ... 2000 MAN STRUGGLES TOWARD MANHATTAN ... HEATH KIRCHART FRONT BLUNTS THE REAL WAY ... ARTO GETS PUNK ... COREY DUFFEL WEARS A TOILET SEAT ...

Arto: More proof that he can do a frontside air

Al Petersen gets psychobilly on the over-vert at Glory Hole. To ollie this high takes guts

Don Nguyen takes the stairs at El Toro. Within the next year, someone is gonna kickflip it

Opposite page: Thrasher hat, Ben Davis, Vans, **Cardiel**, Ripon… We're talkin' epic

My first caption was tack-sharp: "How beautiful skateboarding can be when done correctly." **Hewitt**, frontside crap

Somewhere out there, the best spots go unskated

Left: Some people thought the spot in this photo was computer generated. **Bailey** took us there and earned the cover

Previous spread: I almost lit myself on fire for this pyro stunt, but **Pete Hewitt** was quick to burn the bowl in Hokkaido, Japan

Koston can't be faded

Pine box **Dan Drehobl**

The Palace Steak House serves up catcher's mitt slabs; **Gonz** would end up like both if he didn't make this Kilty McBagpipe

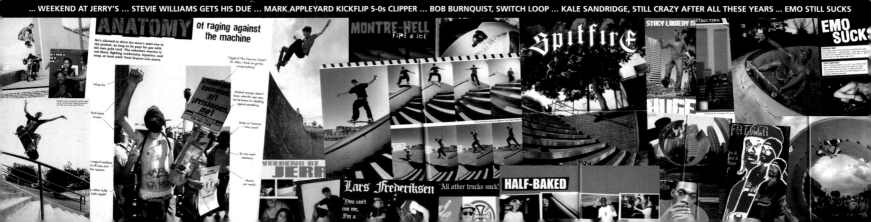

By MARK APPLEYARD

LEGEND:
GEOFF ROWLEY

GEOFF HAS PUSHED the boundaries and raised the bar in skateboarding. He's broken through the doors and brought skating to new levels. The shit he was doing when he first moved to America was unheard of. When Geoff shot his backside 360 cover, he broke his wheel off ollieing into that ditch, then drove 45 minutes to Bob Burnquist's house to rummage through his yard in search of a new one. He found an old dog-chewed wheel, drove back, and did the backside 360 on three 51s and a ragged vert tire. Geoff is nails. I can watch Geoff skate a parking lot and be amazed. He's got it like that, incredible style and originality. Geoff is one of a kind. He's an original, a true fucking ripper.

"GEOFF IS NAILS"

To be honest, **Geoff Rowley** *should* be a millionaire if he does things like this. 180 nosegrind, Wilshire

Daniel Harold Sturt © 2001

2002

"When skateboarding is outlawed,
only outlaws will skateboard."
—*Joseph Stalin*

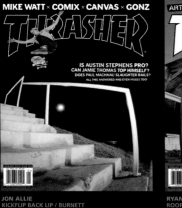

MIKE WATT × COMIX × CANVAS × GONZ

THRASHER

IS AUSTIN STEPHENS PRO?
CAN JAMIE THOMAS TOP HIMSELF?
DOES PAUL MACHNAU SLAUGHTER RAILS?
ALL THIS ANSWERED AND EVEN MOSES TOO!

JON ALLIE
KICKFLIP BACK LIP / BURNETT

ARTO SAARI'S HELSINKI SUMMER

THRASHER

ROB WELSH
DEMO GODS
ZOUNDS CITIZEN FISH
EXHUMED

RYAN JOHNSON
ROOF TO POOL / BURNETT

S.O.T.Y. PARTY MAYHEM

THRASHER

¡PELIGRO
FANTASTICO!
TEMPLETON · CASWELL · STEPHENS

STONED AGAIN
PAPPALARDO · APPLEYARD · SPROUL

ALIENATION VACATION
TIM O'CONNOR · JASON DILL

INFAMY · ZOUNDS
BUTTHOLE SURFERS
MERLE HAGGARD
FLOGGING MOLLY

BASTIEN SALABANZI
KICKFLIP FAKIE / BURNETT

ARTO SAARI × SKATER OF THE YEAR

THRASHER

2 FREE
POSTERS
INSIDE

ALSO: TRUJILLO / CARDIEL / McCRANK / SALABANZI
ROWLEY / BURNQUIST / FOWLER / KOSTON & MORE
+24 STARVING AMS
SNAPPING AT THE HEELS OF LAZY PROS
ZOUNDS: SLAYER / BILLY CHILDISH / SMOGTOWN

ARTO SAARI
FAKIE OLLIE BACK LIP FAKIE / BURNETT

DANGER ZONE: TONY MANFRE SWITCH OLLIES WALLENBERG

THRASHER

SALBA & MOUNTAIN
RETURN TO THE
PINK MOTEL

TAMPA AM
CASWELL TAKES IT
CARRIE GIVES IT

HEADS:
ETHAN FOWLER
NEIL HEDDINGS
CHET CHILDRESS

ZOUNDS:
HAR MAR SUPERSTAR
CONVERGE · DAG NASTY

JASON ADAMS
OLLIE / BURNETT

LIVE TO SKATE · SKATE OR DIE

THRASHER

TAMPA PRO
REYNOLDS · KOSTON · CARRIE

TEXAS PIPE
MISSIONS

ZOUNDS
REDMAN · THE STITCHES
SUPERCHUNK · THE HIVES

DARRELL STANTON
BACK NOSEBLUNT / MORF

100% RAW SKATEBOARD ACTION

THRASHER

RAZING ARIZONA
WITH ED TEMPLETON & THE MULE

TEXAS DAN'S COPING ROUNDUP
RKL CAPLETON MELVINS

JAMIE THOMAS
OUT TO CROOKS / BURNETT

TALIB KWELI · THE BRIEFS · ICARUS LINE · REAGAN SS

THRASHER

TOM PENNY
LOST IN TRANSLATION

FOWLER & CO
ON THE ROAD TO RUIN
COREY DUFFEL
NO TALK. JUST HAMMERS

TOM PENNY
SWITCH 270 FLIP / BURNETT

MARSEILLE · DILLINGER FOUR · MARKOVICH

THRASHER

Gosh That Looks Like Fun...
LIVIN' THE DREAM
Koston · Anderson · Carroll · McCrank
GIRL INVADES EUROPE
PLUS: ATMOSPHERE · PLANES MISTAKEN FOR STARS

ALAN PETERSEN
METHOD / OGDEN

JOSH KASPER: PSYCHO STAIR ATTACK

THRASHER

TOUR CARNAGE:
JAMIE THOMAS
IN BARCELONA

25+
STUPID BITS OF
USELESS
INFORMATION

MIDWEST
MANIACS
DENNIS BUSENITZ, DARRELL STANTON
& PETER RAMONDETTA
RAISE HELL IN THE HEARTLAND

JERRY SMYTHE
FRONTSIDE CROOKS / VITELLO

SKATE SHOCKERS INFECT EUROPE
CASWELL BERRY · AUSTIN STEPHENS · ED TEMPLETON + MORE

THRASHER

EL TORO IS
WASTED AGAIN

HEADS
CHRIS DOBSTAFF
ALEXIS SABLONE
ADELMO JR.

ZOUNDS
THE ROOTS DISTILLERS
BLOODLET NEW FOUND GLORY

DUSTIN DOLLIN
FAKIE FLIP / OGDEN

ANDREW REYNOLDS FOREVER

THRASHER

ENDLESS
SUMMER
ROLLER-BLADES, VERT RAMPS,
BB GUNS, AND ROOT BEER

ANDREW REYNOLDS
FRONTSIDE FLIP / OGDEN

2002

JON ALLIE BURSTS into the big time, grabbing the cover with a kickflip back lip in Chula. Alex Moul kickflips to late-shove over an entire ditch. The Red Dragons continue their tough guy legacy and ams start to take the spotlight, like Austin Stephens who has a full interview. Arto Saari shoots his summer vacation for the mag. Ryan Johnson puts face to floor for his highly controversial Vagabond slam cover. Frank Gerwer kickflips Wallenberg and is king for a day. Andrew Reynolds Cabs the Carlsbad gap. Geoff Rowley's Vans point the way to skate slippers. Peter Hewitt finally gets on Anti-Hero and Oscar Jordan makes it back in the mag. Bastien Salabanzi sparks another cover controversy with his backyard pool kickflip. Grind King predicts the Hubba revolution to come with beat-looking strippers holding their wares. Astoria, Oregon park opens; hot ams include Greg Lutzka, Dennis Busenitz, Paul Rodriguez, Anthony Mosely, Caswell Berry, Billy Marks, Chris Cole, Ryan Smith, Terry Kennedy, Mikey Taylor, and Adelmo Jr. Tony Trujillo spins padless McFlips in Oz. Bootleg skateboards starts a tiny-type battle with Baker and everyone else. Tampa Am coverage is spruced up by Patrick O'Dell's Later'd crew and the addition of an outgoing gal named Carrie. Peter Ramondetta makes the Real roster. DC ads answer the call of the wild with a taxidermy animal series. Darrell Stanton makes his debut on the June cover with a backside noseblunt at Clipper. His follow-up, the ollie over to frontside blunt on the outside, is one of the gnarliest tricks of all time (though not in our mag). Harold Hunter goes flying salami at ASR. Terry is the first kid to leave Baker. Jake and Luke get popped skating pipes in Texas with the creepiest mug shots this side of *True Crime Weekly*. Mongo intervention is detailed. Kevin "Spanky" Long gets an interview before he even realizes he was working on one. Josh Kasper finally owns up to rollerblade rumors—all true. *Sorry* is the vid to get, unless you're watching *PJ Ladd's Wonderful Horrible Life*. Toy Machine lead the way in fashionable haircuts. BMX Jihad is called. Alexis Sablone switch kickflips big blocks. MACBA big four becomes the new proving ground. Tom Penny returns with giant yellow clothing. Skating goes even more ATV. Epic 'crete abounds, and TNT is rewarded the SOTY.

CRONAN

Corey Duffel talked a lot of smack and had the skating to back it up

Opposite page: This is straight Hollywood here. **Ethan Fowler** skates over Aotearoa

OGDEN

TONY BLOWS OUT MARSY ... MIKE SMITH LIVES IN A BARN ... MIKE WATT APPEARANCE NO. 4,080 ... MATT HENSLEY BRINGS HIS SKATEBOARD ON TOUR ... ARTO SAARI TAKES THE BEST PHOTOS OF HIS EPIC SUMMER ...

ANDREW REYNOLDS

"ON THE EDGE OF NOWHERE"

DAWES

Heddings, battered

BURNETT

Being that he just retired, **Alan Petersen** can reflect on the times he wasted Marseilles. Look up, Bailey

Opposite page: **Alain Goikoetxea**, pivot fakie on the edge of nowhere. Mikasa, Japan

Nollie heel to fakie by **Bobby Puleo**.
Australia has it all

SPAIN'S STILL THERE ... THE DUDES IN SLAYER ARE AROUND 40 ... CROOKAHOLICS.COM ... WHAT'S A RAGDOLL? ... ROB WELSH TALKS ABOUT NEWPORTS ... THE BIGGEST PIPES IN HISTORY GET SERVED IN SOCAL ...

LEGEND:
ARTO SAARI

By GEOFF ROWLEY

"LIKE A FINELY SCULPTED PIECE OF RARE FURNITURE"

I HAVE NO IDEA where the bitch is right now so I'll let it all rip while the coast and evening are clear. Many men have entered the realm of professional skateboarding and have been partial, complete, or absolute masters at this game. Many have come and gone, gone and come (defo worse!), and some are even here that you'd wish would just piss off. Some people care, some don't, some thrive on the carnal pleasures of having people and kids look up to them sucking at their every move, awakening and enclosing their souls, eating at their very being, the very reasons why they should skateboard—not for recognition but for the pursuit of personal satisfaction, another way to say "fuck you" to your own soul for doubting you.

Arto Saari is someone who I would call my brother. I think he equally wants to beat me as much as I want to ram his head up his own pipe. I am equally comfortable screaming at him as I am praising him. I would give my right arm to save him, though not my left. I have watched him grow from a young, intelligent brat into a well-rounded, international man of intense humor, all the while growing myself. I would be lying if I didn't say that Arto has taught and helped me as much—or more—as I have helped him. I will always be indebted, on and off the skateboard.

His skateboarding and travels have spoken for themselves, and I believe he is one of the most talented, graceful skateboarders alive. His style and way of riding are of original Finnish origins, like a finely sculpted piece of rare furniture. When he first popped on the scene, current professionals couldn't keep up with him and were worried of his existence.

He was on fire and it showed, especially in videos (*Menikmati*, *Sorry*). It was a four-year blast of radness and I was there for it all. Shit! I was amped by it and would secretly watch the videos when he wasn't around in order to get instantly inspired. It had that effect on me, and I wanted frigging more.

During those years, 1998–2003, Arto went through many travels in life, booze, women, nights of extreme indulgence…and he came out a better person, a man if you will, complete with a shining humor that you just can't buy or learn. Currently he is filming secretly with friends in a way that nobody shall see until the unveiling of the next Flip video. I am more than proud to be his associate and attorney; I am goddamn livid. To the hills, my son! We have work to do.

Arto Saari conquered the world from Finland. He's like a god to some; frontside air proper

New York's all right, if you want to get robbed or murdered. **Dan Pensyl** does both on some spooky mini-ramp

... JOE LOPES, RIP—GREAT SKATER, KILLER DUDE ... GROSSO BLASTS ... CARDS BUSTS OVER BROOKINGS ... TAMPA ASKS CLYDE SINGLETON HOW HE GOT THOSE SCARS ON HIS CHEST ... LUNDRY TRIES TO HELP INDONESIA ...

Lucky, stupid, gnarly… **Frank Gerwer** gets what everybody wanted: A kickflip over the Big Four into history

WALLENBERG'S GREATEST HITS

1990 Mark Gonzales: Ollie

1992 Jesse Paez: Frontside 180

1998 Diego Bucchieri: Backside 180

2002 Frank Gerwer: Kickflip

2003 Tony Manfre: Switch Ollie

2003 Tony Manfre: Switch Frontside 180

2004 Steve Nesser: Pop Shove-it

2004 Lindsey Robertson: Heelflip

2004 Darrell Stanton: Switch Backside 180

2004 Andrew Reynolds: Frontside Flip

2005 Chris Cole: Tré Flip

OGDEN

BURNETT

Jerry Hsu has all the hair he needs

OGDEN

Painted pants won't help front-blunting the bars. **Corey Duffel** fits the gear
Opposite page: Onslow bowl in Wellington, NZ, is, well, Black Diamond territory. **Hewitt** is the right man for the job

Olson and **Hackett** can't accept reality

... LAUSANNE IS GIRL'D OUT: KOSTON RIPS, CARROLL KILLS, BUT CASWELL WINS ... PUNK KNOWLEDGE WINS GUITARS ... BART STILL RIPS ... REYNOLDS FRONTSIDE FLIPS THE BERNAL 16-STAIR FOR A GNAR-BOOTS COVER

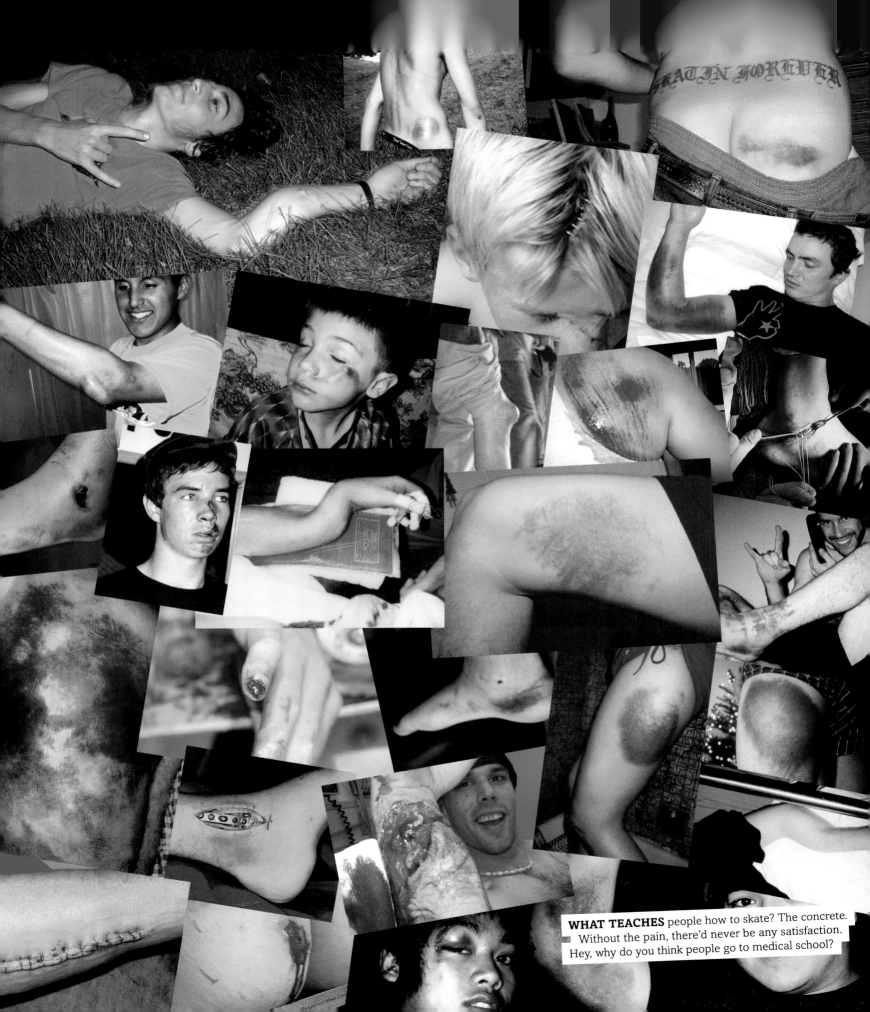

WHAT TEACHES people how to skate? The concrete. Without the pain, there'd never be any satisfaction. Hey, why do you think people go to medical school?

2003

"I've been to the edge...
I got no time to mess around."
—*David Lee Roth*

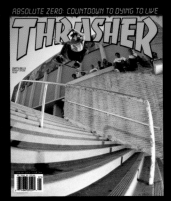

ABSOLUTE ZERO: COUNTDOWN TO DYING TO LIVE

THRASHER

BILLY MARKS
KICKFLIP FRONTSIDE LIPSLIDE / BURNETT

MUSKABEATZ · GOTHAM · UPLAND LIVES

THRASHER

THINGS TO DO IN
TEXAS WHEN
IT'S WET

THE WORST
SKATEPARKS

HEADS:
ZERED BASSETT
JUSTIN ROY

RYAN SMITH
NOSEBLUNT SLIDE / BURNETT

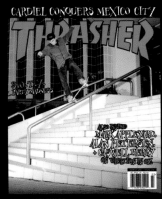

CARDIEL CONQUERS MEXICO CITY

THRASHER

ALSO INSIDE:
MARK APPLEYARD,
ALAN PETERSEN,
& CASWELL BERRY
OR TACKLING IS OZ

MARK APPLEYARD
FRONTSIDE NOSEGRIND / OGDEN

HERMAN, HEWITT, HELL YEAH!

THRASHER

AND YOU WILL
KNOW US BY THE
TRAIL OF DEAD

DOUBLEROCK
THROWDOWN
MARK APPLEYARD vs. CHRIS COLE

BRYAN HERMAN
KICKFLIP / BURNETT

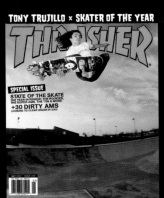

TONY TRUJILLO × SKATER OF THE YEAR

THRASHER

SPECIAL ISSUE
STATE OF THE SKATE
THE YEAR IN REVIEW: THE ROOKIES,
THE SUPER-AMS, THE TOP & MORE
+30 DIRTY AMS
LOOKING TO CLEAR HOUSE IN 2003

TONY TRUJILLO
STALE / OGDEN

$KATE FOR MONEY, DIE FOR FAME

THRASHER

NO HOLIDAY IN THE SUN
BAKER IN OZ

HEADS:
MATT DOVE
JAMES CRAIG
BRIAN SUMNER

RIDE OR DIE:
151 HEARSE TOUR
MIKE HASTIE · JAPANTHER · BUJU BANTON + MORE

HEATH KIRCHART
BACK LIP / POMMIER

HANDSOME MEN, UGLY TIMES IN SPAIN

THRASHER

HAVE A GO!
JOHN RATTRAY
DISCOVERS AMERICA

HEADS: VEGAS · CALES
BOULALA & ZITZER

YOU A WINNER!
SCORCHING AZ SUN, BEAT AZ LAGS

ZOUNDS: HATE ETERNAL
KNOCKOUT PILLS · GZA

JOHN RATTRAY
INVERT / BURNETT

CARNAGE! SKATEBOARD INJURY BLOODFEST

THRASHER

THE HUNT FOR
HENSLEY
IN GOD'S LAND OF HOT BITCHES

EVERYBODY LOVES
LEO ROMERO

NORTHWESTERN
SLACKERS

HEADS:
NATE JONES
LINCOLN UEDA
JEREME ROGERS

ZOUNDS:
AESOP & ELIGH
TURBONEGRO
(SMOG) IMMOLATION

TOM PENNY
KICKFLIP FAKIE / KROLICK

DANNY WAY × MARSEILLE × ZERED BASSETT

THRASHER

INSIDE:
GRECO
GANGSTARR
LANCE MOUNTAIN
SUPERSUCKERS
+ HEAPS MORE

MARK GONZALES
BACKSIDE 5-0 / MORF

SKATEBOARDING IS (STILL) DEAD

THRASHER

BELIEVE THE HYPE

MUSIC
IS DEAD
TOO

GUY IN THE
SKY PHOTOS
SO HOT RIGHT NOW

FASHION
NEVER
FUNCTION.

BURIED INSIDE:
TOSH
'NANDEZ

LOOSE TRUCKS +
LOOSE WOMEN

VEGAS STRIPPERS
& TWEAKER HESSIANS

+ DUFFEL
IN WOMEN'S PANTS

DARREN NAVARRETTE
LIEN AIR / OGDEN

GIRL GONE WILD / ANTI-HERO / ZOO YORK

THRASHER

5 GREATEST
SKATE LIES
EVER TOLD

ZOUNDS:
BORED STIFF
THE SKULLS
AN ALBATROSS
THE FORGOTTEN
CACTI WIDDERS
+ MORE INSIDE

RICK MCCRANK & LANCE MOUNTAIN
FRONTSIDE AIR OVER FRONTSIDE GRIND / MORF

BASTIEN SALABANZI 22 PAGE BLOWOUT

THRASHER

PARTY TIME!!!
SPRING
BREAK
FOREVER
JAMIE THOMAS, CHRIS COLE,
JON ALLIE & THE ZERO POSSE
ROCK OUT ACROSS AMERICA

BASTIEN SALABANZI
FAKIE FLIP / BURNETT

2003

AMS CONTINUE TO point the way with Toy Machine's Billy Marks grabbing the January cover and an interview in which he flips into everything. Zero's *Dying to Live* debuts with a full feature in the mag. Bryan London goes big and then disappears. Chet Childress back Smiths under the backhoe's teeth and Bob Loseedo wears a Speedo. Jim Greco is off drugs and switch three flips 10 stairs to prove it. Dan Drehobl cross-dresses in Texas. Michael Sieben joins the team. Certified Pieces of Suck start to filter in, showing the ugly side of the concrete park revolution. Weiger Van Wageningen has the hardest name and inward heels to nose down rails. Cardiel kills the funky curves of the new Mexico City park. Bryan Herman grabs the cover and a full interview. Peter Hewitt attacks San Diego's new Washington Street park. Jereme Roger's *Yeah Right* ball-crushing sack ad is one of the best ever. Pools become acceptable terrain, even for the cutting edge. Dan Sturt makes the loop, East Coast legend Pepe Martinez RIP, I-Path hits big with Jah and his disciples, and Marc Johnson joins Chocolate. Navarrette buys a hearse and hits the road. We finally get Heath Kirchart in the mag by giving him a cover. Each issue is bigger than the last. Leo Romero passes up the pros to score a full am interview riding for Foundation. Barley's on Birdhouse. Chinese wood sends a shudder through the biz. *The DC Video* hits big with Danny Way's high-flying Super Ramp part stealing the show. Sheckler loses his pads. Chris Cole is gnarly. Danny Way does his first *Thrasher* interview in 10 years. Zered Bassett goes East Coast gnar. Nike makes a big push, grabbing Paul Rodriguez and Brian Anderson—barely a squawk is heard. Chad Fernandez unloads the gnarliest stunts of his career and no one bats an eye. Ultra fresh Anthony Van Engelen flips his script and goes Nugent, officially marking the beginning of a new genre—the tech hessian. The first King of the Road is the most exciting thing to happen to skateboarding since urethane. Deluxe wins(!), but Drehobl's epic machine gun frontside air gets the cover bump. The year closes with a mega-issue featuring Bastien Salabanzi's mind-melting 22-pager and Zero's Spring Break tour. Mark Appleyard nollies into a 10-stair backside noseblunt and is named SOTY shortly after.

MEXICO COMES UP WITH THE VANS TOURS AND CRAZY PARKS ... BOB LOSEEDO STILL WEARS A SPEEDO ... PHOTO JOCK NIK FREITAS IS A ROCK GOD ...

BURNETT

CROMAN

Please kill me, I need the rest. **Gareth Stehr**, showtime

Left: The **Mexican kids** loved watching **Cardiel** blast their park

BILLY MARKS SCRUBS IT IN THE ALLEY ... JIM GRECO COMES CLEAN ... YEARBOOK PHOTOS SELL HELLA PRODUCT ... *MUSKABEATZ* GET BENCHED ALL OVER LA ... PIGS OVERREACT AT ZERO PREMIERE ...

DIRTY BILLY
COMES CLEAN

MUSKABEATZ

ON ALL DIFFERENT ELEMENTS

NEW
TACTICS
FOR
LIVING

SKATE FOR MONEY
DIE FOR FAME

JIM GRECO IS OFF DRUGS!

SHREDDING

BOWLED OVER

FOR HEDD

BAKER

GEAR
CRISIS

REACTING TO the rodeo clown-like pant explosion of the early '90s, a new breed led by trendsetters Ethan Fowler, Ali Boulala, Jim Greco, Jamie Thomas, Tony Trujillo, and Jason Dill decided looking like a frat boy on wheels wasn't for them and began adding leather jackets, scarves, fedoras, bandanas, slam bracelets, beards, shades, tattoos, white

"LOOKING LIKE A FRAT BOY ON WHEELS WASN'T FOR THEM"

belts, blouses, and, most surprising, skin-tight trousers to their on-board attire. Fantastic haircuts ranging from mohawks to jet-black emo mops soon sprouted wildly. Kids unable to find jeans tight enough (or too embarrassed to peruse the aisles of the Junior Miss department) took to ripping seams and picking up needle and thread. And when Krew released their ultra-slim Andrew Reynolds jeans they became an instant best seller. Though some may fault this latest exuberant experimentation for its excesses, it's better than looking like every other dork at the mall. —*Mike Burnett*

Timmy Garner is down for life. Deck snap over the love seat in The Valley
Opposite page: Tennis is for Duffers. Switch snaps are for **Chris Cole**

... DOCTOR Z IS SKATING LIKE MENTAL ... DANNY WAY'S BANANAS. HEELFLIP 360 OVER 60 FEET? FOR REALS ... FAUSTO TALKS ABOUT INDY, 25-YEARS DEEP ... SKATESPOT LIBERATION ARMY GOES PRIME TIME ...

Caswell Berry grew up skating in San Jose, so he knows how to ride to the bar

LEGEND: TONY TRUJILLO

By NEIL HEDDINGS

I GUESS I CAN UNDERSTAND everyone's infatuation with this dude. Honestly, I get butterflies in my stomach every time he rolls up. Some sick shit is going to go down. He's one of those fools who seems to have it all: hesh, hair, garage band, beer breath, and my wife even says he's "really cute." Basically, the kid's got style and he fucking rips. He's a natural. I don't think I've ever seen him give any forethought to any run he's ever taken. Throw up the horns, put the beer down, and let it all go.

I remember he flew in late to some contest I was at in Ohio. You know how dudes spend their entire practice sessions trying to get that one run down, doing the same thing over and over again like it's the fucking Olympics? Tony showed up right before his run was called—no practice sesh, the aforementioned beer breath, some jet lag, and I think he even had fluorescent pink griptape. Whatever, 'cause he did a sick run. It was fun as hell to watch; put everybody to shame, and a big smile on my face. His run told me to just go skate. Fuck it, have a good time. Skating's not supposed to be that serious.

I wish I could have grown up skating with that kid; I just know it would have made things a little different. Better. It always made a difference when he showed up at Burnside in Portland, OR. This young fuck from NorCal opening up new lines all over the park that us locals never thought of. Instead of being bitter, it's more natural for skaters to just freak out. Start screaming and yelling and slapping our tails on the coping. It's the kind of positive energy created by a sick motherfucker celebrating life on a daily basis through skateboarding. I love skating; it's carried me through all the goods and bads in my life. It's carried me through jail today. What's cool is to see someone like Tony carrying that shit around in his back pocket, keeping it safe and real. So check it out: turn up the metal, pass the bottle, and drop in. That's Tony in my eyes. Much love, man.

Tony Trujillo is the last stand of real deal skating. Pillar pillage at FDR

"THROW UP THE HORNS, PUT THE BEER DOWN, & LET IT ALL GO"

Bryan Herman goes for the distance on this *Amazing Race* crooked grind

The Three Stooges: **Gareth Stehr, Johnny Layton,** and **Adrian Mallory** tag team some stairs in Miami

Frontside flippin' **Dustin Dollin** is on a roll

Assault Vehicle Supreme **Dan Drehobl** takes it personally in Minnesota

Opposite page: **Rick McCrank** can do 'boarding like this front hurricane all day

... SID "THE PACKAGE" ABRUZZI ALWAYS POINTED THE WAY ... KOTR IS OFF & RUNNING ... SESSION AT DENVER PARK: AWESOME ... PHARES DFL ... TEAM DLX BURNS WESTWARD TO VICTORY

2004

"No hands, no grabs,
no crybabies."

—*High Noon at the Big Four*

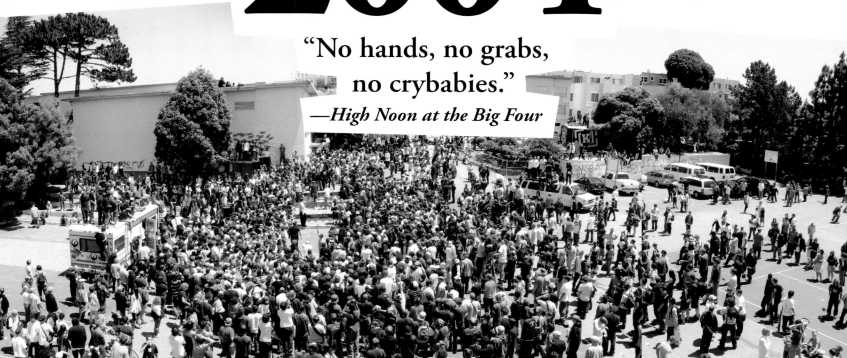

SPECIAL KING OF THE ROAD ISSUE
DOLLIN vs KOSTON vs TRUJILLO vs McCRANK vs FOWLER vs PJ LADD + MANY MORE

THRASHER

20 AMAZING SKATERS / 15 DAYS ON THE ROAD
15,000 MILES / 4 MYSTERY GUESTS

**HEAD-TO-HEAD
ACROSS AMERICA**

THE COVER
THE CASH
& THE CROWN
1 TEAM TAKES IT ALL

TONY TRUJILLO
FRONTSIDE ROLL-IN / MORF

JOSH HARMONY | FISCHERSPOONER | BULGARIA

THRASHER

15 THINGS
YOU COULDN'T CARE
LESS ABOUT INSIDE

HEADS
STEVE ROCHE
& AARON ARTIS

ZOUNDS
DEVIL MAKES THREE | SINCE BY MAN
NEW STRANGE | C-RAYZ WALZ | + MORE

JOSH HARMONY
NOSEGRIND / BURNETT

SKATER OF THE **YEAR** PARTY BLACKOUT

THRASHER

OREGON ESCAPE PLAN
**APPLEYARD
ELLINGTON
MUMFORD
& BARTIE**
(POST TOUR DEPRESSION SESSION)

TOP SECRET:
**BOLT CUTTER
PROJECT** REVEALED!

MATT MUMFORD
CRAIL SLIDE / BURNETT

MARK APPLEYARD | SKATER OF THE YEAR

THRASHER

FREE POSTER
APPLEYARD vs
TOM PENNY

SPECIAL ISSUE
THE STATE OF THE **SKATE:**
THE ROOKIES | SUPER AMS
UNKNOWNS | EPIC 'CRETE
DANNY WAY | SHECKLER
TRUJILLO | & MUCH MORE

ANTI-HERO: THE MOVIE
CARDIEL | HEWITT | BAILEY
STRANGER | GERWER | + ONE DIRTY HIPPIE

MARK APPLEYARD
TORQUED-OUT LIEN / BURNETT

TAMPA AM | SOUTH AFRICA | JUNK JAM

THRASHER

HATE ON THIS
**DOBSTAFF
INTERVIEW**
18-STAIR BLUNTSLIDES
HEELFLIP TAILSLIDES
TRIPLE SET SWITCHFLIP
& HELLA MORE INSIDE

CHRIS DOBSTAFF
BLUNTSLIDE / SCURICH

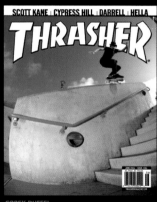

SCOTT KANE | CYPRESS HILL | DARRELL | HELLA

THRASHER

COREY DUFFEL
BACKSIDE LIPSLIDE / BURNETT

MODEST MOUSE | MACHNAU GOES COCONUTS | PHX AM

THRASHER

**GRINGOS
EXTREMOS**
SPANKY HEATH
HERMAN & LEO
IN COSTA RICA

ERNIE TORRES
FRONTSIDE FLIP / BURNETT

FREE JAMIE THOMAS POSTER INSIDE
EXCLUSIVE 26-PAGE JAMIE THOMAS CAREER RETROSPECTIVE - THE PHOTOS, THE INJURIES, THE VIDEOS, & MORE

THRASHER

EXTRA! EXTRA!
**WALLENBERG
MURDERED!!!**
WHO GOT WHAT • WHO GOT SERVED?
REYNOLDS! BAQUELI! LINDSEY! COLE!
FULL DETAILS INSIDE

JAMIE THOMAS
WINDOW RIDE / SHIGEO

MEN AT WORK: ETNIES DOWN UNDER

THRASHER

FAHRENHEIT 540
**20 YEARS OF
THE TWIST**
AS TOLD BY McGILL, HAWK,
BLENDER, HOSOI, TRUJILLO,
GROSSO, DREHOBL, LANCE,
KOSTON, CARDIEL +OTHERS

26 DAYS LATER'D
BAKER BUS
REYNOLDS, SPANKY, HERMAN, & CREW
RAISE SOME RUCKUS ACROSS THE U.S.

GEOFF ROWLEY
50-50 / BURNETT

JON ALLIE | CAIRO FOSTER | ALEX MOUL | HELMET

THRASHER

TOY MACHINE vs
MIDDLE AMERICA

AUSTIN STEPHENS
KICKFLIP / BURNETT

LOPEZ INTERVIEW | SPEEDEALER | RDS

THRASHER

IMMATURE AMATEURS:
WINDSOR JAMES
LENNY RIVAS
TONY TAVE

ZOUNDS:
SMUT PEDDLERS
TOM WAITS

CHAD BARTIE
BLUNTSLIDE / BURNETT

SPECIAL KING OF THE ROAD SUPER ISSUE

THRASHER

4 SICK TEAMS
15,000 MILES
20 AMAZING SKATERS
HEAD-TO-HEAD
ACROSS AMERICA

TEAM ZERO

CARNAGE IN
CARBONDALE

KING OF THE ROAD

TOMMY SANDOVAL
BACK LIP / SHIGEO

Bastien Salabanzi is all grown up when he clips this fakie three down the flat four. Money

Opposite page: Knocking out his teeth or knocking out bonelesses, **Peter Hewitt** is a rare breed. Pizzey's not for pussies

2004

GNAR IS THE WORD for 2004. Josh Harmony makes another am cover and interview. Skate fashion widens with ultra-tight Joey Ramone pants, fanciful hats, and wild hair becoming common. The bolt cutter contest takes the trophies straight to the streets. Oregon concrete crusades become common, even for top street pros. Garrett Hill and Tommy "Die Trying" Sandoval join Zero. Skate Coach tells it like it is. *Tent City* warns of retarded tent occupants. Rhino and crew reap the benefits of the devastating Cedar Fire with some new San Diego holes, Volcom invades South Africa, and Darrell Stanton finally gets his big interview. Beardo uncovers Baja 'crete. Mumford splits from Zero to start Legacy, Trainwreck starts Young Guns but boards are never actually produced. Nyjah Huston is the first micro rail-ripper, jumping on big bars at age nine. Mullen's Tensor Globe shoes marks the first in a bizarre cross-branding trend. Corey Duffel dresses like a sideshow geek and 180s 21 stairs. Tulsa's Ernie Torres grabs the cover with a double set frontside flip crusher. Leo Romero turns pro. Phoenix Am is the new Tampa. Chris Miller shows he still rips and there's no hard feelings. Red Kross introduces another new genre: the young old guy. Jamie Thomas gets the 10-year retrospective treatment. The Wallenberg contest is marked by socked-up TWS photogs, hidden hip pads and, most importantly, Andrew Reynolds unloading the finest frontside flip of all time. Bob drops for some bizarre looking Hurley kicks and goes sky diving. The McTwist turns 20 and Grosso explains. Shane Cross is the latest Australian surprise. Tony Tave goes both ways on a flawless switch kickflip back lip contests. Beardo's Channel Street park puts some Burnside in LA. Rincon is hot, *Freedom Fries* is the hot Euro vid. Emerica goes Wild in the Streets in NYC. Bryan Herman turns pro. Jon Allie and Adrian Lopez get interviewed. Lee Dupont adopts Tony Tave, Windsor James and Lenny Rivas for the Circa team. Herman 360 flips Wilshire 15. 2004 ends with the King of the Road, starring Girl, Real, Zero, and Almost. Zero wins, Koston shines, and the mid-way Carbondale Run event is the most epic ever. Following the release of his DC *Deluxe Addition* footage, Danny Way is the only choice for Skater of the Year—the first guy to win it twice.

GRECO IS IN GEAR AND CRISIS MODE ... CARDIEL BREAKS BACK, GETS KICKED OUT OF REHAB FOR BEING TOO INSPIRATIONAL ... WE CALL OUT ALL HEADS FOR A WALLENBERG BASH ...

Tommy Gunz came straight out of Chula Vista and proved not to fuck with the real Diego. Fat 180

Opposite page: **Omar Hassan** can claim the first no-pads 540 in a backyard pool. Vagabond was hot like the sun

LEGEND:
MARK
APPLEYARD

By MATT MUMFORD

THE NAME MARK APPLEYARD is as important to modern day skateboarding as the maple leaf is to the Canadian flag. You simply can't have one without the other. And to be quite honest, Canada needs to be as proud of Mr Appleyard as they are of their beer. He's played an undeniable role in the way people look at the level of professionalism in skating today. Mark has always pushed the limitations and boundaries of progression in the skateboard world. He's quickly become one of the most recognized and respected skaters of all time.

With his well-rounded parts in the infamous Flip vids *Sorry* and *Really Sorry* to *Thrasher* dubbing him Skater of the Year and ranking him number one on numerous readers' polls, we seem to have learned to always expect the expected from Mark, and it appears there's still much more to come. Yet with everything he's accomplished, he still manages to carry himself with the honest humblings of an Average Joe, which Mark is certainly not.

Skaters worldwide admire him, and amidst his peers he's considered an attribute and inspiration. His free flowing attitude reflects in his effortless style and natural ability, making him one of the true masters of the game and undoubtedly one of the most notable skaters of all time—leaving him etched in the archives as one of the greats. Quite simply, when it comes to skateboarding, Mark Appleyard is like a four leaf clover. They only come along once in a lifetime.

Mark Appleyard redefined the image of the dirty skate rat

"LIKE A
FOUR LEAF
CLOVER"

MAPSTONE

Cardiel slaps into a frontside 5-0 in Denver, CO, truly burning to ride

Josh Harmony nosegrind, and a confirmation of his faith

There were all these weird missions where Paul Shier, Kenny Reed, **Jerry Hsu**, and Patrick O'Dell would be busting in Brato-Slavia and hooking up with 18-year-old ex-commie lags. Switch 180 to frontside 5-0 to fakie

HIGH NOON

The Big Four is around six- and a half-feet tall and 17-feet long. Jamie Thomas told me it's like the Santa Monica triple set plus 10-feet of distance. If you go 30-feet past the bottom of the Santa Monica triple set, you can buy a "Got Sand? Venice Beach, CA" T-shirt and a Miller Lite.
—*Michael Burnett*

Reynolds Frontside flick for cash

Top: Many are called, few are chosen

ZERO
PRESENTS
THRASHER MAGAZINE'S
**HIGH NOON
AT THE BIG FOUR**
THE FIRST EVER
**BIG TRICKS
CONTEST**
"THE TRICKS HAVE BEEN CALLED
& THE MONEY'S UP FOR GRABS"
BACKSIDE FLIP · $1500
FRONTSIDE FLIP · $1500
SWITCH BS 180 · $1500
THREE FLIP · $2000
SWITCH FLIP · $3000
NO GRABS   **NO** HANDS
BIG FLIP · $????   FS 360 · $????
PHELPER'S CHOICE · $????
NO CRYBABIES
BRING YOUR GUNS OR STAY HOME
SUNDAY MAY 16th
MASONIC BETWEEN GEARY & TURK · SF
1 HOUR ONLY · NOON TO 1PM · RAIN OR SHINE
PARAMEDIC ON DUTY
INVITE ONLY

This is the ultimate Anatomy photo: **Weiss** not filming, **Ortiz** getting the ass shot, **Mic-E** getting a beer, **Morf** thinking about skating, and **Lindsey** heelflippin.' **Corey Sheppard** in an I-Path shirt?

... ALLIE CARVES HIS NAME INTO MY DESK, I CARVE MINE INTO HIS KOTR TROPHY ... SOUTH AMERICA ... BAD SKATEPARKS ... COSTA RICA ... 20 YEARS OF THE 540 ... DREHOBL KNOWS HE SUCKS ...

JON ALLIE

CLASS 5 RAPIDS

BEERS, BOWLS & BARNEYS

"Tell them I'm Filming!"

FAHRENHEIT 540°
20 YEARS OF THE TWIST

TV ON THE RADIO

MIKE BURNETT, OLLIE DISASTER ON A CLASSIC BACKYARD MINI

ΛΗΑΤ THRASHER MEANS TO ME

AS A KID, *Thrasher* was the instruction manual for a life that seemed bigger and better than the one I was stuck in. It was a lifeline to a world where the streets were lined with quarterpipes, punk bands played in every basement, and dudes with names as far fetched as "Lester Kasai" and "Lance Mountain" blasted 10-foot airs above fantastic ramps and pools. The skateboard world was as big as the Vision Pro Skate Escape and as small as a ditch contest (in nearby Pflugerville, Texas!). I studied each new mag like the Torah, and, after breaking my leg in eighth grade, memorized all the back issues too, thanks to an older skater who lent me his prized collection.

"A WORLD RIFE WITH ADVENTURE AND OPPORTUNITY"

As an adult working for *Thrasher,* I imagine kids like I was and try to provide them with all the important things I remember about the mag—wild photos, a few laughs, and stories about the people, both famous and underground, who make skateboarding so special. I'm not sure if there are skaters who pour over *Thrasher* the way I did (what with the Internet and the Bam and all), but if there are, I want to show them that world—a world rife with adventure and opportunity, but one that they can only get to by riding their skateboard. —*Michael Burnett*

BURNETT

The new kids never knew the darkness, and it shows with monster shit like this. **Ryan Sheckler** is already Fortune 500
Opposite page: **Adrian Lopez,** find a need and fill it

SPANK DOG GETS JUMPED IN ... TOMMY GUNZ FRONTSIDE FLICKS THE SHIT OUT OF SD FOR THE COVER OF 13 ... DOLLIN ONLY OLLIES ON VERT ... CHAD BARTIE ROCKS THE CRADLE ... KENNY REED IS PURPOSELY ALOOF ...

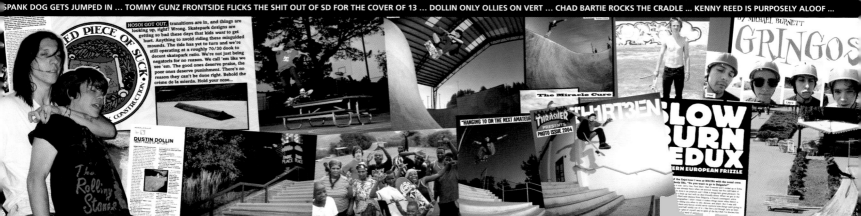

Tony Tave color corrects a textbook switch kickflip back lip. He earned the roll away shots

BURNETT

Daewon blunts to fakie on a very harsh "get hurt"

Mandatory dude for the Zero Juggernaut, **Chris Cole** is single-handedly writing his own ticket book. Switch pop shove-it, two KOTR trophies, and a SOTY trophy? Damn

Opposite page: **Eric Koston** went on King of the Road twice. The first time was "kinda fun," the second time he came to win. Countdown back noseblunt

Tony Trujillo said, "Fuck Skater of the Year. I'm King of the Road!"

... ALL ROADS LEAD TO CARBONDALE ... THE TEAMS CAME FROM BACK EAST, WE MET 'EM IN COLORADO ... BEER, GUNS, FIRES, BLOOD, AND BEATDOWNS? PRETTY MUCH, LIKE, EPIC ... ZERO, GIRL, ALMOST, REAL

WARPED TOUR CASUALTY

The Bay Blocks scene ain't what it used to be. The ...

SUCKER PUNCH: JASON JESSEE
the worst thing is MY KID scout got to witness the beat down of HeR papa other than that I lost weight. LOVE JASON

DIVER DOWN
Remy Stratton dons the headgear needed to survive the stench emanating from a recent Black Flys bowl bust.

COLIN McKAY AND ASHTON KUTCHER, DRAGONS FOR LIFE. WHERE'S SHECKLER?

SPANKS: WHEN YOU'RE A JET, YOU'RE A JET; FROM YOUR FIRST CIGARETTE TIL' YOUR LAST DYING BREATH, YOU'RE A JET

"Only the mediocre are always..."

"I still haven't found what I'm looking for."

RIBALD RABIES

Dog Boy doesn't get his name for eating dooks. He gets it from canine corruption.

Bobby Puleo: What me worry?

HOT DOG
A very young Rodney Mullen poses in front of his air-conditioned dog house. Ah, the good ol' days.

"DUDE, YOU ROCK"

"NO DUDE, YOU RULE"

TRASH

THE VERT VAMPIRE AIN'T PACKING SILVER BULLETS

RUSSIAN DENTISTRY
Rick Howard and Marc Johnson dig for the tooth fairy.

HE CAN CONCEIVE IT. HE CAN BUILD IT. HE CAN RIP IT. DENNIS BUSENITZ IS THE NEW GENERATION. FUCK BUCKFISH, WELD A FLAT BAR

SEPARATED AT BIRTH
Passing the 'King of Trim' torch, Vinny Vegas and Hugh Hefner are maxin' and relaxin' in Hollywood

GETS HITCHED DATELINE: Easter Sunday, 1991.

THE NAME of the mag is *Thrasher*.
The page that hurts the most is called Trash

HUNGRY FOR PARTY FAVORS, ED DEVERA

2005

"I remember skaters for what they've done for skateboarding, not for what they got out of it."

—*Guy Mariano*

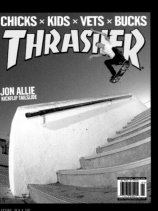

CHICKS × KIDS × VETS × BUCKS

THRASHER

JON ALLIE
KICKFLIP TAILSLIDE

JON ALLIE
KICKFLIP FRONTSIDE TAILSLIDE / MORF

15 MOST LOVED SKATERS AND THE FIVE MOST LOVE-STARVED

THRASHER

HSTOKED
THE JERRY HSU STORY

HICKS WITH STICKS
FRESH ARKANSAS 'CRETE

ONLY CRIME

MR VEGAS

RUNE GLIFBERG
BACKSIDE OLLIE / BURNETT

ADVENTURE IN SOUTH AMERICA

THRASHER

PAUL MACHNAU
20 PAGES OF
TOTAL GNARLICIDE

THE USED 'CRIME IN THE CITY'
ELECTRIC FRANKENSTEIN

PAUL MACHNAU
BACKSIDE TAILSLIDE / NICK SCURICH

THRASHER

GEOFF ROWLEY
...OUT FOR BLOOD

ROAD DOGS
THINGS TO DO
IN AUSTRALIA
WHEN YOU'RE DEAD

NEUROSIS
BURNING BRIDES
THE RAPTURE
ANGRY AMPUTEES
KEV KELLEY + MORE

GEOFF ROWLEY
360 OLLIE / STURT

SKATER OF THE YEAR ★ DANNY WAY

THRASHER

YEAR IN REVIEW:
MARK APPLEYARD
ZERED BASSETT
DARRELL STANTON
CHRIS COLE
BASTIEN SALABANZI
PAUL RODRIGUEZ
MARK GONZALES
PAT DUFFY
CHAD MUSKA
JAMIE THOMAS
T-EDDY AWARDS
MEPHISTO PREDICTS
& TONS MORE

DANNY WAY
SWITCH CROOKED GRIND / STURT

50 PAGES OF UNPAID BRUTALITY

THRASHER

MAKING FRIENDS DOWN UNDER
PAUL RODRIGUEZ
WIEGER / REESE
SUPA / DOLLIN

BANANA FARM FREAKOUT
MINUTEMEN VALLEY 'CRETE
SHREDDING FOR HEDDINGS

PAUL RODRIGUEZ
SWITCH FLIP 50-50 / BURNETT

NECK FACE VS PETER RAMONDETTA

THRASHER

DEAD IN JULY!!!!
~~APPLEYARD~~
~~SALABANZI~~
~~GLIFBERG~~
~~CHALMERS~~
~~BODZALA~~

HEADS
~~LEO ROMERO~~

GO DEMON
OR
GO HOME

OH YOU SKATE?
WHO CARES.

ARTWORK BY NECK FACE

SKATE COACH × HIGHTOWER × FLORIDA

THRASHER

**TOSSERS
IN TEXAS**

**CONSOLIDUDES
EN MEXICO**

ANTHONY VAN ENGELEN
SWITCH CROOKS / BLABAC

JIM GRECO LIVES!!! DUSTIN DOLLIN DESTROYS NYC IGGY POP

THRASHER

FOURSTAR JAPAN
HOWARD GONZALES
KOSTON CARROLL
SCHAAF ANDERSON
PJ LADD & EVEN GUY MARIANO

RICK HOWARD
BACKSIDE OLLIE / MORE

★ DANNY WAY ★ MADE IN CHINA ★

THRASHER

LAKAI RUSSIA
MARC JOHNSON
CAIRO FOSTER
MIKE CARROLL
RICK HOWARD
& JB GILLET

18-PAGE INTERVIEW
★ ERIK ELLINGTON

ANTI-HERO BURNS EUROPE UNSEEN
15 MORE THINGS YOU COULDN'T GIVE ANY LESS OF A CRAP ABOUT

ERIK ELLINGTON
BACK LIP / BURNETT

GUY MARIANO IN HIS OWN WORDS +14 PAGES OF FLIP **CREATURE** BACK FROM THE GRAVE

THRASHER

GREG LUTZKA
MIDWEST MARAUDER

SCOTLAND A FAIRY TALE LULLABY BY JOHN RATTRAY
RDS PARTY TOUR + TONS MORE

GREG LUTZKA
BLINDSIDE FLIP / SCURICH

ZERO vs. FLIP vs. HABITAT vs. ELEMENT

THRASHER

4 SICK TEAMS
20 AMAZING SKATERS
HEAD-TO-HEAD
ACROSS AMERICA

100+ PAGES
OF INSANITY!

CHRIS COLE AND TEAM ZERO
WALLRIDE / SHIGEO

2005

JON ALLIE OPENS the year with a kickflip front tail down Clipper. Toy Machine gets back in the video fray with *Good and Evil*. We show you how to thrash through the ages. The Cayman Island's massive Black Pearl skatepark opens just before a record-breaking hurricane season. Vanessa Torres scores a full interview and calls out the competition. Nyjah Huston's Hollywood 16 feeble borders on child endangerment. O'Dell interviews Duff McKagan and can finally quit. The 15 Most Loved skaters of all time are revealed. Photogs get their cameras confiscated in SoCal. Darrell quits Real for Plan B— restarted with Danny Way, Colin McKay, and Paul Rodriguez. Adam Alfaro becomes Tony Alva. Rowley cork screws a 360 ollie into the murderhorn for our latest, most controversial cover and kick starts the ditch and bank skating revolution. Phelps flips a car in Oz dressed as a priest and lives to tell the tale. Reynolds nollie Cabs Carlsbad. The new Blind vid had *Video Days* hidden in the extras and Jake Brown is vert reborn. We finally get a P-Rod cover but have to go all the way to Australia to do it. Jake Duncombe is an Ozzy mullet maniac. DVS' *Skate More* puts Daewon in everyone's top five. Street elitist Rob "Wu" Welsh busts a vert handplant ad. Chris Cole three flips Wallenberg. Omar Hassan busts a Washington Street 540. Terry Kennedy is back on Baker just in time for the *Baker 3* vid. Hosoi is out and blasting methods in the combi. Zero's *New Blood* video hits big, with Jamie Thomas finally passing up last part for Chris Cole. Dennis Busenitz wins Tampa Pro. Arizona is the new California. The Vans combi hosts a pro event with Chris Miller taking the Masters. Greco spills the beans on recovery. Erik Ellington gets an interview and the cover with the best ripping of his career. Danny Way almost dies jumping the Great Wall of China. Guy Mariano bounces back to top form with a full feature and Greg Lutzka frontside 270s to backside noseblunts down rails. The 2005 King of the Road features Zero, Flip, Habitat, and Element, and is our wildest adventure yet. Zero wins again and Chris Cole is crowned the MVP. He goes on to earn SOTY status. Skateboarding is the gnarliest and best it has ever been.

Tubular vision: **Greg Piloto** gets kinda dyslexic

The foot of Polk Street has seen tons of stunts, but few as fat as **Peter Ramondetta**'s ollie out of the grandstand

BABY NYJAH WINS TAMPA AT 10 ... GEOFF ROWLEY SAYS "WE HAVE THE GNARLIEST TEAM, HANDS DOWN" ... DANNY WAY ACCEPTS HIS SECOND SOTY TROPHY—THE GUY IS THE MOST AWESOME SKATER SINCE IT STARTED ...

"FLIPPIN' CARS BEATS FLIPPIN' BURGERS"

Danny Way crooked grinds a jump ramp on steroids (not him, the ramp)

Navarrette? Must be a crail. Dream spot, Cayman Islands

Paul Machnau noseblunts 18-deep at age 28. Live forever

GUZMAN'S NUTS ... IT'S THE WEB, STUPID ... EVERY ROCKSTAR SKATED "BACK IN THE DAY" ... CARDIEL, SACTO, BITCH ... FLIPPIN' CARS BEATS FLIPPIN' BURGERS, JUST ASK THE VICARS ... RALPH AND REESE ARE BROS ...

VANESSA TORRES TELLS 'EM WHERE TO PUT THEM SKATE STOPPERS. FRONT BOARD. PHOTO: DOUBT

SK8 STOPPERS

AS THE IMAGE of skateboarding in the new millennium reached new heights of popularity, the act of skateboarding itself reached new lows of tolerance. Now that Grandma knew about skating from her TV, she certainly didn't want any of those hooligans jumping around in front of her house. Neither did the head of security at the bank downtown, or the mayor who

"THESE UNSIGHTLY ITEMS OF HATE WERE SOON FASTENED TO ANYTHING WITH A 90-DEGREE ANGLE"

had just okayed the construction of the skate/bike/blade park at the soccer fields, or the city planner who just completed the new public square. And so an entire industry based on putting an end to the public nuisance of skateboarding was born. Suddenly, a lot of long-standing spots were ended with a few ugly metal blobs being heavily bolted into the edges of ledges everywhere. But it didn't end there—these unsightly items of hate were soon fastened to anything with a 90-degree angle to it, creating a sea of zipper-looking benches and ledges in every self-respecting 'burb. Beyond that, architectural companies began producing plans with skate-stopper functions built into the design before any marble could be grinded. Street skating literally got clamped down on in the '00s, but of course skaters found their way around the problem, as we always do. Grinders, sanders, Bondo, and the time-honored truck bashing process were employed, and when a skate-stopper needed to be removed, it was. —*Mark Whiteley*

STURT

Sherlock Holmes and Doc Watson would be hard-pressed to get a clue on **Geoff Rowley**'s frontside truck bash. Nice veins
Opposite page: There's not much to do but sit down when **Tony Trujillo** puts his game face on. Fat Algorta channel frontal

... HOLMES IS FREE, TAKES FLIGHT ... TK BACK ON BAKER ... SKATE COACH GOES OUT FOR REVENGE ... GERWER BABY? LET'S PRAY IT CAN'T HAPPEN ...

More **Dustin Dollin** amplitude. This spot is, unfortunately, now ruined. Kickflip wallride to fakie, up the drunks

Seth McCallum, feeble fakie deep in Mex

Cairo back lips in Russia

Stu and **Div** double up Livi. True skate beasts

... GRECO COMES BACK TO EARTH, LEAVES SHORTLY THEREAFTER ... L RON HUBBA WHEELS? ... ANTI-HERO MAKE ENEMIES IN FRANCE AND AUSTRIA ... TNT TELLS THE FRENCH PRESS, "MMD: MOURNING MARSEILLES' DEATH

LEGEND:
BASTIEN SALABANZI

By SALMAN AGAH

GROWING UP SKATING in California is a trip. I have found in all of my travels that California-bred skaters have a hypersensitivity to style and fashion. Blame it on Hollywood or rock and roll or entertainment all together. Whatever the case, that sensitivity has permeated itself into the fabric of skate culture. And quite frankly, I'm glad.

The first time I met Bastien I was in France in the mid '90s. I read somewhere recently that Rune Glifberg discovered this wonder prodigy. That very well may be the case, but I'd like to think otherwise. See, being on the Vans Warped Tour for a few years I had the luxury of traveling around the globe, meeting lots of skaters on the fringe. So when I was in France it surprised me to see this waist-high kid showing all of us what time it was. I proceeded to plead with Steve Van Doren from Vans to not only sponsor Bastien, but to help him come to California. The rest is history.

Back to my point. Since the first time I saw Bastien skate I knew he was special. Why? Because it's not always what tricks you're doing or can do—it's how you do them. Bastien knew this intimately. That's why being as small as he was then—in my eyes, and obviously in the eyes of many, including the most scrupulous of critics, Geoff Rowley and the Flip squad—Bastien was a giant, a master, and a culmination of all the very most desirable characteristics of a pro skater. Bastien exudes power, confidence (which can be mistaken for cockiness), balance, grace, and individuality in a way that makes him extremely influential and unforgettable. In the annals of skateboarding history you can be sure that if Bastien has the poise, determination, and guidance to continue in his personal rise to the top he'll be a bright light to up-and-coming skaters everywhere whom have a love for skateboarding.

The bottom line is that when you come from the Congo and then to France and finally to America and the eyes of the whole skateboarding industry and community knows who you are globally, friend, you have arrived. Now that's a story to be told. Bastien forever.

Foot extension flick front nose. **Bastien** has a deep, deep bag

"CONFIDENCE (WHICH CAN BE MISTAKEN FOR COCKINESS)"

Arto frontside pick in Santa Fe. The wall, the sky, go time

Trent Reznor's doppelganger, **Garrett Hill**, switch varial flips for The Eagle

Opposite page: **Tosh Townend** hippy jumps in the land of the animals. The eyes never lie

Creepy **Stefan Janoski** flips to fakie, and into Habitat's second place

... KOTR: "THE BEAST CREEPS EAST" ... FOR THE RECORD: ZERO, HABITAT, FLIP, ELEMENT ... LOUISVILLE IS THE MEETING PLACE FOR MYSTERY GUESTS BARBEE, KNOX, DRESSEN & DANFORTH... PHELPS LIGHTS A KID ON FIRE

SOMETHIN' ELSE
"THE BOY SPED ACROSS THE WHEEL-WORN FLAT BOTTOM, TRAVERSING THE TRANSITION UP TOWARDS THE LIP OF THE RAMP.
THE DOG SAT BACK, POISED AND MOTIONLESS, AWAITING THE PRECISE MOMENT TO SPRING FORTH AND SNATCH THE FOUR WHEELED VEHICLE FROM BENEATH THE BOY'S FEET.
THE MOMENT..."
Joe Lopes and friend at his backyard ramp.
TUFF GUYS WHO SKATE
december
somethin' else
THRASHER
SOMETHIN' ELSE
Skeletal Dynamics
ON YOUR KNEES
Somethin' Else
DOWN TIME
hole shot
I SHOULD BE ABLE TO BIFF ONE OF THESE GUYS... DIE! DIE! DIE!
JUST ONE MORE STEP (SNICKER)
DAMN! WHERE'S THAT STUPID CONTACT LENS?
ATH OF PHYSICS
ghout skate history the four-wheeled artisan has often
nself victimized by the ever-present perils of his craft
Somethin' Else

SOMETHIN' ELSE

SNACK TIME

ISOMETHIN' ELSE

Somethin' Else

ISOMETHIN' ELSE

Little Rascals

METHIN' ELSE

Somethin' Else

ISOMETHIN' ELSE

SOMETHIN' ELSE

Somethin' Els

BETTER THAN A KICK IN THE HEAD

GEARIN' UP TO GET DOWN

WATER YOU TH

METHIN' ELSE

SOMETHIN' ELSE

METHIN

Somethin' else

Somethin' Else

KING ROD

SOMETHIN' ELSE

"THE STOKE on the way out" is how the mag is supposed to end, but like everything else in life sometimes you just gotta say "Fuck it"

WE ALL KNOW ANDY MAC GETS "HIGH" SKATEBOARD-

Wide Load

SOMETHIN'

BIG RIG

The cycles of skateboarding run hot and cold. When it's hot, watch it on TV. When it's cold, put on some gloves and bomb a hill. We've been in the game through three ups and two downs, and like **Matt Mumford**, we'll continue to be here until the dust and bearings run dry. *Thrasher*: 25 years of Skate and Destroy. What you got?

SKATE & DESTROY is Dedicated to the Love, guts and Intensity that
John Cardiel gives to skateboarding. With the EYES of an Eagle and the heart
of a champion, this kid has kept it real for all to see. Check the tracks.
Much Love from the Thrasher Familia JAKE PHELPS
HRC
2005